Voices of Recovery from the Campus

Stories of and by College Students in Recovery from Addiction

Lisa Laitman, MSEd, LCADC
Linda Lederman, Ph.D.
Irene Silos, MPA, SC-C

Editors

Voices of Recovery from the Campus

Editors

Lisa Laitman, MSEd, LCADC

Linda C. Lederman, Ph.D.

Irene M. Silos, MPA, SC-C

Printed by CreateSpace, an Amazon.com Company

Requests for permission or further information should be directed to:
Linda C. Lederman
linda.lederman@asu.edu
or
Lisa Laitman
llaitman@echo.rutgers.edu

Acknowledgments

We want to thank all of the authors, specifically, Megan, Alberto, LB, Karen, Lara, Joe, George, James J., Heather, Cynthia, Tim, and others, who took the time to put their stories in writing and to share their experience of campus recovery. Without them, this book would not exist.

We also want to acknowledge all of the students in recovery who have taken a newcomer to a meeting when an ADAPS counselor asked, stayed up with someone in the Recovery House when he or she was having a difficult time, or helped to celebrate a birthday or an anniversary, because recovery will always happen one day at a time and one person at a time.

Table of Contents

Acknowledgments ....*iii*

About This Book *1*

Forward *3*

Preface *5*

Overview *6*

Chapter 1 – My Story and I'm Sticking to It *9*

Chapter 2 – A Flick of the Switch *18*

Chapter 3 – AA Ruins Your Drinking *25*

Chapter 4 – Not the Smoothest Guy on Campus *37*

Chapter 5 – The First Drink *43*

Chapter 6 – Life is Good *55*

Chapter 7 – A Cut Next to the Rest *65*

Chapter 8 – My Bottom Brought Me to the Top *72*

Chapter 9 – Hey – Wake Up! *75*

Chapter 10 – Smart in School *87*

Chapter 11 – I Never Identified *101*

Chapter 12 – Ha-Ha We Have Her Now *105*

About This Book

Lisa, Irene, and I refer to this book among ourselves as the *Little Book,* even though we officially titled it *Voices of Recovery from the Campus.* Its first edition was a labor of love, as is this one. The first edition was created after the 20th Anniversary Reunion of the recovery program at Rutgers University in 2003. Rutgers was one of the first schools in the country to create programming to help students in recovery to stay sober despite the culture of college drinking in which they found themselves.

At the reunion, person after person rose to tell the story of what it was like to be a drunk in college, what happened to get sober, and what sobriety is like these many years later. Their stories, like most of the stories of recovery told in AA meetings across the country and world, were powerful testimonies of the struggle of addiction and power of recovery.

What makes these stories different from many of the stories you can hear in the rooms of AA and other 12-step programs that deal with addiction is that all of these stories began in college. The people whose stories appear in this book did not drink themselves out of jobs, homes, and marriages; they began their recoveries early enough to avoid the years of tragedy or early death that awaited them.

Like all recovering alcoholics, these writers have a disease, a disease for which there is no cure, but for which there is a daily remission. Like all recovering alcoholics, they had caused damage to themselves and others until they found the courage to replace drinking with a life of sobriety.

The purpose of the first edition was to put together stories written by recovering alcoholics who had attended the 20-year reunion, and then share those stories with others who were currently in the recovery program at the university and graduates of that program.

Now, 10 years later, there is a growing recovery movement, sparked by the work at Rutgers University, Augsburg College, Texas Tech University, and other pioneering recovery programs for college students. Hundreds and hundreds of colleges and universities across the country now have some type of program designed to help students in recovery achieve and maintain sobriety and complete their education.

Yet, there are thousands of college students who want to get sober but do not know that there are others their own age who are struggling with recovery. They may feel what one of the recovering alcoholics at the reunion described as *terminally unique*: a feeling of wanting to be sober in what seemed like "the sea of alcohol on the college campus." As a result, we decided to create a second edition of the book and distribute it widely.

This book is written for you if you are in college and concerned about your drinking or staying sober; if you are a friend, parent, brother, or sister of someone in recovery (or who wants to be); or if you are simply someone who wants to know more about what it is like for a college student to come face to face with his or her own drinking and decide to stop *one day at a time.* It is written by people in recovery who wanted to tell their stories to help others know what it is like to live with alcoholism and the daily reprieve of recovery. And it is written to speed you along the way if you are one of those among us who fight this life-threatening disease.

Linda C. Lederman, Ph.D.

Arizona State University

May 2015

Forward

May 1983, in some respects, seems very long ago but, in others, it was like yesterday. That was when I was hired at Rutgers University to start the Alcohol and Other Drug Assistance Program for Students (ADAPS). I remember thinking that maybe I should not take the job because it was just me; they were hiring one alcohol counselor for 50,000 students! When my boss told me that he was not sure there was enough work at Rutgers for one alcohol counselor, I got even more worried.

However, I was young and energetic (and idealistic), and I did know one very important thing: recovery was possible. In my prior years of working in traditional treatment programs, the average age of clients who came for help with addictions was early 30s. Their stories were those of lost careers, underemployment, divorces, broken families, estranged and misguided children, poverty, physical health problems, and personal losses. When I was told that the mission of the Alcohol and Other Drug Assistance Program was early intervention, I knew this was where I was meant to be. Forget the ratio of 1:50,000. This was a chance to cut off the inevitable consequences of continued drinking that I had witnessed for years.

The stories in this book are the tales of the young people who have become my life's work. I have lived through the struggles of which they write in these stories, and I am very grateful to have been trusted with their lives.

I thank those of you who have committed your very personal stories of recovery to paper here. It is invaluable for those not yet in recovery or for those who are still struggling in early recovery. The addict cannot (and need not) do it alone, and I, as an alcohol/drug counselor, also cannot do it alone. I rely on the courage, strength, and hope of others in recovery and a staff of committed counselors to help me with those new young people who are still coming in every day, 32 years later.

Lisa Laitman, MSEd, LCADC
Rutgers University
May 2013

Preface

Irene M. Silos, MPA, SC-C

The creation of *Voices of Recovery from the Campus* stems from a desire to bring together stories from recovering addicts who began their recovery either just before entering college or while in college in hopes that those who are currently in that position can have a resource to which to relate.

Attempting recovery from alcohol and/or other addictions while trying to remain in college has its own, somewhat unique, challenges. Compiling stories from people who have successfully accomplished this helps to share that experience, strength, and hope with others who are just beginning the journey. The goal of this book is to bring you, the reader, stories that you can relate to, being a college student in recovery. These stories present the hardships, sorrow, struggles, and pain that young college students endured before finding recovery and go on to show the joy, peace of mind, confidence, and success they have achieved since attaining recovery. Stories that help you to know that you are not alone, that the pain and uncertainty you may be feeling has been felt by others, and like others, you, too, will make it through.

Since 1983, when the Rutgers Recovery Program began, there have been over 100 students who have gone through the program, a very high percentage of whom are still sober today. The writers of the stories wanted to share with you their strength and hope.

May you find something in these stories that will help you to stay on the road to recovery and achieve a wonderful, successful life.

Overview

Linda C. Lederman, Ph.D.

As a professor of communication who is interested in recovery from addiction and relapse prevention, I am especially interested in college students and the challenges they face in their recovery from alcoholism and other drug addiction.

Recently, I had the privilege to work on a project that focused on the drinking behavior of college students and the role of communication in that behavior. I worked on the project with Lisa Laitman at Rutgers University, who founded the first recovery housing program in higher education in the country. Through Lisa, I learned of the hundreds of students who had been in the recovery program at Rutgers over the last 20-plus years. I was honored to be invited to the 20-year reunion of the Rutgers Recovery Program in 2003. What struck me as most interesting was seeing and hearing the men and women, some in their 20s, others in their 30s and 40s, tell stories that began in early childhood and progressed to dorms, frat houses, and coffee shops on or near the college campus, where many first decided to try to get sober, and how hard it was for so many of them to be in the rooms of Alcoholics Anonymous (AA) as college students who were getting sober when most of the people they saw in the rooms were often much older. I found myself thinking that the "Big Book" of AA and much of the AA literature focus on recovery later in life. They include such topics as family life and losing that family; job and careers and the loss of those; and the typical life circumstances of the 30-, 40-, or 50-year-old's attempting recovery. These circumstances are so different from the circumstances that face the 18-, 19-, or 20-year-old college student that it might make it hard for them to fully identify. With alcoholism/addiction's being the cunning, baffling, and tricky disease that it is, the inability to identify can be a real roadblock to recovery and may be just what the disease needs to convince the most full-blown, fall-down addict that he or she "isn't so bad after all."

From these thoughts, the idea of this book was born. The goal was to ask people who had begun their journey of recovery in college to tell their stories in the hope that these stories might make it easier for current college students who are beginning their recovery to identify with. Each story in this volume was written by a person who began his or her recovery during his or her college years. These stories share each author's experience, strength, and hope. It is a book of stories written by people of various ages now, but who all began their recovery journey during their years in college. Their tales tell of different events and situations, but all include what it was like to be in college while trying to deal with alcohol abuse and recovery from it. It is a book written for college student alcoholics and those who want to understand them, by recovering alcoholics who began their recovery during their college years.

The stories differ in the particulars, but there are themes that these stories have in common. All of the stories are written about the college experience and the role of addiction and recovery. They are written by people who got sober/clean and continue to stay sober/clean and tell of the struggles along the path to recovery. Each author gives witness to the reality that his or her life without alcohol/drugs is far better than the life he or she had as a slave to alcohol/drugs.

These are their stories, and they should be told—not because they are particularly dramatic, but because they are stories of ordinary people who did extraordinary things as they fought their addiction and found their recovery from a disease that takes more lives than it spares.

May this book of stories give you the hope you need as you travel the path toward recovery from addiction and attain your success. At that time, maybe you, too, will want to add your story to this collection: to share your struggles, successes, happiness, and sense of well-being that flows from being sober/clean one day at a time.

You, through your story, will be able to share your experience, strength, and hope with others who have a need to identify with those who approached recovery in their late teens and early 20s while attending college. This book is dedicated to all of the brave people who found recovery from addiction and a new way of living.

Chapter 1

My Story, and I'm Sticking to It

. . . she came from a large family and started drinking with friends in her early teens. College was a time of good grades and lots of drinking until she found AA; she has been in recovery ever since.

I guess I have a story that begins like a whole lot of other people in the rooms: I was born into a big Irish Catholic family. I am the youngest of seven children, and I loved that. I think it was all pretty normal, except that my father had a pretty bad temper, drank a lot, and we lived on top of a funeral home. That said, everything was fine until I hit about twelve. I remember being VERY anxious; don't know why, I just was. I didn't notice at the time, but when I started drinking here and there with friends when I was thirteen and fourteen, I calmed down some. We all were trying alcohol then (at least I thought we all were), but I think I liked it more than others right away. I would drink at parties, football games, and over my friend's house when her parents were not home. We would drink whatever we could get our hands on, stealing from our parents' liquor cabinets and putting all the booze of the same color in a jar and hiding out and chugging. Yes, not surprisingly, I threw up a lot.

It went on like that for a few years. My friends and I got better at obtaining booze, enlisting the help of older siblings and investing in fake IDs. When I was 16, my mother was diagnosed with melanoma, skin cancer. She started to go to New York for experimental treatments, and suddenly I was home alone, a lot. Everyone had either moved out or was in college except my dad and one brother, who was busy in law school. This was terrifying; remember that my dad scared the hell out of me. And I was learning that alcohol helped ease my anxiety and fear.

So I began to drink alone. After school and softball practice, I would come home, open a diet soda, add some whiskey from Dad's cabinet, and begin to cook dinner. I wanted to be the woman of the house. When my mom was home, she was so tired. She never asked me to change or grow up; she acted like it was all fine, even while she threw up every morning while making my breakfast.

I was 17 and a senior in high school when my mother died. I think I was afraid to drink too much because I was afraid of losing 'IT.' But I do remember during the repast after the funeral, some of my older sisters pulling me aside to give me some alcohol to . . . I don't know, feel better? After that, I drank alone all the time, daily. I stole alcohol from the cases of booze my father had in the basement, or I convinced someone to buy it for me, or later I got a great fake ID using my sister's birth certificate (I think the DMV still has her as two inches shorter and with blue eyes instead of brown).

I got a boyfriend, so I had to start drinking vodka so I wouldn't be detected. I know now that vodka stinks, too, but for some reason he never called me on it. I worked as a waitress and went home and drank every night the summer after my senior year. I started to drink to feel normal. I learned how to keep a level of intoxication during which I could function. Then at the end of the night, I stopped going to bed and just started passing out in front of the TV.

I had done well in school in spite of the chaos, and it was time to go to college. My oldest sister, who was my godmother, took me to school, which was one state away. That was okay with me; my dad was having a lot of trouble getting over my mom's death, and he still just made me nervous.

I loved college! I did pretty well in school, never below a 3.0, and drank with abandon. That was the job of a college student, wasn't it? But not everyone drank like I did, so I was able to tone it down during the week. Through most of my college career, I just drank on the weekends—all weekend.

However, every summer or break, I went home and resumed my daily drinking. Each time I went back to school, I would bring half a gallon of vodka and hide it in my closet, until I got back into the swing of my weekend drinking. I remember always "forgetting something" and running back to my room, chugging some vodka, then catching up with the girls to go to dinner or out to a bar.

As the years went by, my drinking increased. I had a fake ID and began going to different liquor stores to drink secretly. I remember the feeling of relief I would get when I knew I had a half of a gallon of vodka and would be set for a bit. I also remember the anxiety of running out and scrounging around for ANYTHING to drink. Once, at home, I remember drinking the Crème de Menthe my father put on his ice cream, just for a buzz.

I was definitely becoming two people. I was a college student who had friends, did well in school, and was active in the campus ministry. I was also a person who needed to drink before she went out to do anything, especially drink. Now I think about how much work it was to keep it all going, and I wonder how well I could have done in school if I had been sober. I wonder, but I don't regret.

The summer after my junior year, I went home and worked two jobs. I would go in and waitress at a lunch place, then I would come home, have a few wine coolers, and be a hostess at a pizza place. I was 20 years old and feeling like I couldn't keep it together anymore. My siblings had caught me a few times with bottles in my closet or a full glass of booze in my room. I lied some more. I had one friend who, every time I got in her car, said she smelled alcohol. I told her I had just used mouthwash. I think I eventually just convinced her that Scope smelled like straight vodka. I remember feeling very tired. I also started smoking cigarettes about a year earlier, and hid that from my family as well.

I turned to our parish priest, who had helped me

tremendously during the death of my mother. He was a young guy who made time for me. I told him how much I was drinking. By then I knew it was a problem and had poured out my stash once or twice only to panic and restock. He took me to the alcohol- and drug-counseling center at Rutgers. I started seeing a counselor, who eased me into the realization that I was an alcoholic. She hooked me up with some other college girls, who took me to an AA meeting in downtown New Brunswick. I immediately compared myself to these older women at the meeting with all their complicated problems and began to feel better. I wasn't in such bad shape compared to them. So, of course, I kept drinking. I spent that summer going to meetings, getting a few days together, and going back out. In the back of my mind, I kept thinking that I had to drink on my twenty-first birthday and at my wedding. I ended up on the bathroom floor of the Knight Club Bar on my 21st birthday with, I believe, a concussion. The longest I was able to stay sober was 13 days, then it was the fall, and I was back to Villanova.

Now I knew I was an alcoholic, so I drank with serious determination. I knew the end was near, but I was putting up a good fight. I began to hang out with a different group of friends, the ones who went to the local pub every night. It didn't take long for me to hit bottom, racing downhill at this speed. That October, I went home for fall break and made arrangements to check myself into the inpatient rehab in the Hurtado Health Center at Rutgers. Two nights before I left school, I drank half of a fifth of vodka and told some of my roommates the plan; the next night I drank the other half and told the rest. I called my oldest sister and told her, too, she said, "I think I have the same problem," and didn't mention it again.

I told my father I was taking the train back to school and began walking to rehab. In true non-coincidental fashion, my priest friend drove by, picked me up, and brought me to rehab; he even visited later. I had to sit in this room by myself for a day; they said it was the detox wing. I didn't have any horrible symptoms but, boy, did I feel lousy. I went in pretty hung over.

It wasn't long before I started to feel things again, and ugghh, that was tough. I had been numb for years. Suddenly, I was anxious again, I had some panic attacks, and I did not know how to be social—sober. I remember just feeling so raw. And I also thought I was damaged goods and would never have a "normal" life. I had a roommate whom I thought hated me. In all fairness, she was mean at first. But I think we discovered we were in this together and started to open up. She is still one of the people I am closest to today.

They made us go to AA and NA meetings while there. I remember we would always go to this Friday night Mine Street meeting, which I loved because it had tons of young people. But one night they celebrated their group anniversary, and it was a party atmosphere. I freaked out and couldn't talk to people sober; I ended up crying by myself in one of the rooms downstairs. I was literally socially retarded; my social skills had been stunted.

After three weeks of rehab, I went back to college and kept myself busy. I went to counseling and found local AA meetings. I even got a sponsor, though I didn't call her. I kept in touch with the people from home in AA and was relieved to graduate and get back there. I had a great summer, hanging out with my old rehab roommate and other young people in AA. And I spent five weeks backpacking through Europe, even hitting some English- speaking AA meetings when I was feeling nuts enough. (I had a bad habit of being motivated only by pain.)

When I was younger, I had always wanted to save the world. In the midst of my drinking, I forgot all those aspirations just trying to keep up with the lies. The next year, I volunteered to teach school in a small Catholic inner- city school in San Antonio, Texas, with an organization called VESS (Volunteers for Educational and Social Services). I promised myself I would put down roots and commit myself to the sober community down there. An old cowboy named Raymond picked me up when I called Intergroup and started driving me to meetings. He introduced me to a girl named Rachel (who was even younger than me!) and suggested I may want to ask her to be my sponsor. I

13

did, and we began working the steps together. I made friends, joined a home group, and celebrated my first year sober in Texas. It was wonderful, and I began to understand that you get out of AA what you put into it. I started to become a responsible adult who actually had the confidence to take care of myself. At the end of my volunteer year, I thought about staying. I suspect now that my family was afraid to have me so far away, and two of my sisters drove down and picked me up. It was a long and quiet drive back. Suddenly, I didn't know where I fit in my family anymore. I didn't want to be the irresponsible baby of the family that was my traditional role.

It was a difficult transition. My family did not really understand AA or my sobriety, and I did not make much effort to help them. I reconnected with my AA friends and had a great time living sober. In the beginning, I really stuck with the women and learned a lot about myself. Of course, it wasn't long before boy met girl on AA campus. Unfortunately, I was sober one and a half years and turning 23, and the boy in question was 35 and had a whopping 30 days sober. To this day, I do not know what I was thinking. I really thought he was much healthier and more knowledgeable than I was. I fell in love hard. In my defense, he was really cute, and I had the self-esteem of a woman sober one and a half years.

It was only a few months later that my boyfriend relapsed, spurring me on to confess my love and begin my quest to save him. This phase lasted a REALLY long time. My family became disgusted with him, and then me. (It may have been the time he called my dad drunk and asked him for my hand in marriage . . . and $1,000; he was a little strapped for cash at the time). I began to pull away from them. They blamed him, but it was also because I was trying to figure out my role within the family as a sober adult.

I also started to let go of my connections with the women in the program. I thrived on the chaos. Eventually, after enough pain, I called the women and they listened to my pitiful tales of self-inflicted pain. It took six years of on-and-off craziness to finally end that relationship. There were times when he stole my car (his sponsor helped me steal it back) or called me, drunk and lost in the middle of the night in New York. There were times I went looking for him and then eventually realized he would find his way back to me whether I wanted him to or not. Throughout the craziness, I kept up with meetings and the fellowship of AA. They saved my butt. Did I mention I don't like to change until I am in a lot of pain?

Actually, my boyfriend did get sober, while we were broken up. When we tried it again, both sober, it didn't work. I learned that you can love someone, but it doesn't necessarily mean you should be in a relationship with him. I believe he is still sober today, and he is on my Ninth Step list. It turns out I wasn't the perfect martyr girlfriend of the chronic relapser—I played a role in the relationship's problems as well.

Around that time, when I was about five years sober, my oldest sister was diagnosed with lung cancer. It was an incredibly painful time, and it was also my call to rejoin the family as a sober adult. I am grateful that I was able to truly be there for my sister at that time. I bought her groceries, drove her to family stuff, and hung out and listened to her fear. I even quit smoking, although I did not pressure my sister to quit. She drank heavily and smoked until she died two years later. I have no regrets about my relationship with her in those last years. I was able to show up. I told her I loved her, and I was with her the moment she died. That is the biggest gift of the program I have received: the ability to show up for life on life's terms.

The women in the program rallied around me again during that incredibly difficult time. I don't remember ever having to be alone if I didn't want to. The day after she died was the big Soberfest picnic; someone sent a card around, and everyone wrote their support. (Except a few people who didn't read it well and congratulated me on an anniversary, which is when cards usually get passed around.)

So as life went on, I kept receiving all the gifts of the

program I never thought I could have. I got a good job and a car, and eventually I even bought my own condo. All the while, I kept going to meetings. Sobriety was no longer something I did; it became part of who I was. Eventually I met another guy in the rooms of AA. This time I made sure he had a few years sober. He laughs at me now because, in the early days, he would tell me all the things he liked about me, and I told him I was just so happy he was sober, had a job, and paid rent. We got married and went on a wonderful honeymoon in Greece, where we hit an AA meeting. I was 31 when we got married, and now I am so grateful that I didn't wait 10 years to get sober so I could drink at my wedding; I really did not miss it!

I began to enjoy my family again and even got close to my father. I know now that he loved me in the only way he knew how. He never stopped drinking, but I was able to connect with him and learn to like him as well as love him. My husband helped me to see him in a different light, without fear. I learned to enjoy his stories and his sense of humor. He died one and a half years ago at the end of a fun family vacation. I think that is the best way someone can go, with everyone you love around.

I almost want to end my story there. Life got really good, I felt comfortable in my own skin . . . I would even say I had some honest-to-goodness serenity. Then I got pregnant and had a baby, and I lost my mind! No, really; I kind of did. I have been blessed most of my life with feeling predominantly sane. Sure, there was the anxiety when I was younger, but it did not prepare me for post-partum depression/anxiety! I bring this up because I think it is important to remember that sometimes we need more than AA. I contemplated medication but ended up feeling better with counseling. I know there are many, many people out there who need both outside counseling and sometimes psychiatric medications in order to reach their own level of serenity. I hope they find it.

I should also mention that my chosen profession is that of a therapist, and I specialize in those who struggle with addictions.

After 9/11, I was fortunate enough to run a program especially for those affected by the disaster who were suffering from substance abuse and posttraumatic issues. I consider myself so blessed to work in a field that fulfills me.

So that is my story, and I am sticking to it! My Higher Power, whom I comfortably call God, has led me along this journey. I have been sober for over 14 years now. I do not do it all perfectly (my sponsor moved seven months ago, and I am still in search of a good one; I call lots of women in the rooms in the meantime), but I try and do the next right thing. I still go to about three meetings a week. I sponsor four women, whom I have come to love and who have become a part of my life. I have a great, sane, sober husband and a wonderful son who has been to more meetings than most 90-day celebrants! I believe that I am truly living the gifts of sobriety, and it all started with a priest who led me to the office of the Rutgers University recovery program director, who pointed me the rest of the way.

Chapter 2

A Flick of the Switch

. . . he was outgoing and active, and the student professors loved him. On the outside, he looked like what every college student should be.

Everybody loved me. I simply rocked. I ran the newspaper, I produced all the concerts on campus, I was in a band, and I had tons of friends. Professors invited me to their homes just to get to know me. I regularly juggled several girlfriends. If there were a profile of what a college student should have looked like on the outside, it was me.

Things are never what they seem, however, especially people. Any closer inspection of me, and my psyche would have revealed something slightly inconsistent: an anxious, scared, nervous, uncomfortable little boy who could barely rise above his miserable self- image and go about his day. I had become a master, with the aid of alcohol, at completely masking the troubled young man inside and appearing acceptable and successful in all outward appearances.

I was a full-blown alcoholic, and things were slowly starting to fall apart. At 22, it all came to a head in the substance abuse office at the Rutgers University Health Services facility. But I am getting ahead of myself. The trouble started long before that.

There is nothing really remarkable about my childhood. I grew up in a small suburban town in Bergen County, New Jersey. My parents were professionals, and we were middle class. We didn't have a lot of money, but I was never aware of any money issues. Although my parents argued frequently, and at the time I thought it was uniquely tumultuous, you learn as a grown-up that most families have their share of stormy weather, and just because your parents fought, it doesn't really make you special. I have one brother who is five years younger; we never really got along. Now we do. Then we didn't.

From my first memories as a little boy, I always had an insane obsession with whether or not people liked me. I was consumed with whether or not I was good enough— whether I measured up. I spent years in therapy as an adult, dissecting where those feelings of inadequacy came from. Learning the contributing factors was helpful, but I discovered that it mattered less than whether I had risen above the poor self-image. As a boy, it was devastating, though. My peers would taunt me in ways that kids do, and I would just put my head down and believe it. Even in writing this, it hurts to think about. I believe those feelings, combined with what I believe to be a genetic proclivity and probably a touch of fate, created a time bomb. The bomb exploded in 1986, when I was 13. It was September. I decided to take a drink one day.

From that very first drink, there was never anything normal about my drinking. None of it made sense. My parents had gone out for a walk, and I compulsively decided I simply must try to drink the whole gallon jug of wine on the table. No reason. No occasion. I just walked over and started downing it! Well, the rest of that episode is somewhat predictable. I was really slogged for the next five or six hours and vomited all over the back yard and got caught and everything . . . the usual lectures and grounding ensued. But what was completely bizarre was that I could not wait to do it again.

That day, I believe I flicked an invisible switch within me. I entered high school that fall. I drank liquor in the house after school just about every day by swiping from my parents, grandparents, the neighbors whose lawn I mowed, the veterinarian for whom I worked—anywhere. This continued all through high school. I got extremely adept at being drunk just about everywhere, all the time!

I went to an all-boys Catholic school, really had few friends, and no opportunities to meet any girls. Other guys were getting invited to parties, they were dating, they were coming in on Monday with stories of crazy weekend trips, they played sports . . . I just went home, and when I was home, I would drink every chance I got.

By the time I left for college at Rutgers, I had become a survivor. I had figured out a coping mechanism to rise above the tremendous feelings of inadequacy and alienation by drinking myself into oblivion all the time. Orientation weekend at Rutgers was my first experience with a true college party—Newell apartments on Cook—and, man, had I arrived! Flick switch number two.

To this day, I will remember that evening as my first real social experience that involved alcohol. The scared kid exploded out of his shell and suddenly was talking to women, having fun, playing drinking games, and singing all the drunk sing- along college anthems (Brown Eyed Girl, Sweet Caroline. I am not dating myself; those will be eternal classics!).

It is important to note that not every experience I had that involved alcohol was a negative one; the parties were fun. Some were simply awesome. Some involve memories that, to this day, make me cackle with laughter. The problem is that I never really knew they stopped. I just kept going and going and going . . . right through, past Sunday into Monday morning . . . right through the different evenings of the week with a different set of friends each night . . . right through the wee hours of the morning into the next morning and an 8:00 am class . . . right into the next weekend . . . right into summer, sophomore, junior, and senior years, right up to graduation . . . stumbling on stage to get my diploma from the dean. I never stopped.

Graduation terrified me. Deep down, I knew that I was going to have to confront some pretty serious demons if I ever stopped to catch my breath. I figured I had a shot at extending the party if I went to graduate school, so I entered a Master's program and began a fellowship, working in the Public Relations department of a giant pharmaceutical company. This was where the tide changed once again. Flick switch number three.

Graduate school was nothing like undergrad. The lightweights had all been weeded out. The ones who went out drinking after class were the hard-core ones. The professors I drank with were the true drunks. Drinking took on a new face and new meaning. I was no longer a kid; I was a grown-up who was trying to survive in the real world, and I was once again scared to death. I thought about my time at the bar just about all day long. I now formed my social circle around those who were drinking as much as, if not more than, I. If a girl I liked wasn't really a drinker, I didn't exactly spend a lot of time pursuing her. Eventually, the hassles of dating, family relationships, and simple friendships proved such a burden that I just let it all deteriorate, feeling eternally put upon and terminally unique. I began to look forward to my time after work, when I could be alone. I just didn't want to be bothered. I would stop at the liquor store on the way home from work and buy enough for that evening; by not stockpiling for the week, I gave myself the illusion that this was no big deal. I would drink from the time I got home until the wee hours of the morning. I would sign on the Internet and talk to strangers in a drunken maniacal tone. My roommate, my best friend for five years, began to hate me and contemplate ways to gracefully end the lease.

I decided to try to get as far away from myself as possible and took off to Alaska on what was officially supposed to be a "research trip" for my Master's thesis. I had no idea what I was doing; I just needed to leave. On a layover in Chicago's O'Hare airport, I pounded cocktails in the airport lounge. I then fell down in a blackout on one of those conveyor belt, people-mover contraptions under all the crazy neon lights. In this pre-9/11 world, this type of behavior was common in airports, so Security simply looked at my plane tickets that were on the floor all around me and put me on my connecting flight. I woke up in Anchorage.

21

Those last 14 days of my drinking were simply the worst. I had to meet a team of people in the Outback and had completely run out of liquor. I figured I would back off for the duration of the trip, since I was supposed to be "focused," and would resume once I was back home. That was when the shaking and the sweating started. I was 100 miles from the nearest town, let alone the nearest bar. I felt so sick I couldn't think straight. I told everyone I must have the flu, and I think some of them may have believed me. The professor in charge of the excursion, however, having had firsthand experience with alcoholism, knew better. He spoke rather directly with me. "When you get back to New Jersey, you may want to think about seeing someone to talk about your drinking; perhaps professor Mitchell." I felt insulted and relieved simultaneously. Screw this guy! But deep down, I knew he was right. The morning I arrived home I went directly to a therapist I had been seeing for a while on campus for "depression" and told her I thought I may want to look at my drinking.

After telling her that I could not stop drinking no matter what I seemed to try, she breathed a sigh of relief and said, now that I finally told her, she could do something. She told me not to move from her office, picked up the phone, and called the Alcohol and Drug Assistance Program for Students' campus director. I went directly to her office, which was at the other end of campus, located in the student health clinic.

While waiting outside for my intake, I started to leaf through some of the pamphlets that were on a table, picking up the famous "44 Questions" pamphlet. I began to check a lot of *yes* answers; I never drank while pregnant, so that was a freebie. Upon finishing, I averaged out my score to a 67%; that was a D+, so, in my mind, I passed. I didn't read the fine print at the bottom, which said that, if I answered any more than a few of these questions as a *yes*, I probably have a problem with alcohol.

I honestly believed that, after a meeting with this counselor, I would have a brief lecture-type session where I could take away tips on how to manage my drinking, and my life and my alcohol intake would suddenly get better and become under control. The concept of alcoholism had not even crossed my mind; I was too young, too smart, and too important to be in throes of alcoholism. I could not possibly be an alcoholic.

But at the conclusion of my session with the director, she looked at me and, in a very gentle but very direct manner, said, "We are talking about alcoholism here." Those words ring so loud and clear nine and a half years later. I was enraged, yet I felt this enormous sense of relief, as if a weight had been lifted from my chest. Would I have to go away to one of those rehabs I used to see on network after-school specials? She explained further that, just because I was in college and a young person, I was by no means immune to addiction. I knew she was correct. Despite my adolescent consternation, we worked out a treatment plan. It was recommended that I attend inpatient rehab, but after howls of protest about how the laws of physics did not apply to me, we settled on an intensive outpatient program of individual counseling sessions, group therapy, and aggressive attendance at campus AA meetings.

My treatment involved meeting other recovering students who lived at Rutgers. Surprisingly, it involved meeting professors at campus AA meetings with whom I had classes. "We have been waiting for you," they would say with a chuckle. It involved constant social gatherings of students in recovery. Rutgers had created a recovery program tailored completely to the life of the student. In listening to other students describe their experiences with addiction, I heard how it affected their class work, their housing situations, and their struggles to stay in school and fit in. These aren't the problems of adults. They are the problems of those of us roughly ages 18 to 24 who are in the early stages of a chronic disease. None of us had to leave school; we went on with our lives with a new bent toward recovery.

Pivotal to successful treatment of the young alcoholic is an effort to teach students that there is life after drinking and that they can and will survive and have fun at the same time. Luckily, I didn't have to drop out of school to get sober. I went from a world where everyone around me was drinking constantly to a world of support, hanging out where people weren't drinking but teaching each other to lead sober lives—and, yes, still acting like college students and having fun.

The people I met in AA and the campus rehab who were going forward in their new sobriety became my circle. Some became friends; one became my wife. I still see most of them every week at campus meetings, where I am still a group member.

Sobriety, at that time, gave me tools to become a productive and useful adult. Getting sober at a young age was the greatest gift that college ever gave me. I even graduated on time. My academic studies prepared me for my chosen field, but sobriety taught me the most important thing: how to live.

I never lost a house, a job, or a spouse, got arrested, or got a DWI, but there is not a shred of doubt that all of those things were on a list of terrible events that would have been my story had I not sat down in fall 1995 and listened to those words, "We are talking about alcoholism." Instead of the checklist of wreckage that is so common after a lifetime of drinking, I have a different list. I am a husband. I am a father. I have a job that I love, that I can't wait to go to every day. I own my own home. I own my own car. I do some things well, and others not so well, but I have such enormous happiness in my life today because I had a choice in my recovery school: that of a life of recovery.

Chapter 3

AA Ruins Your Drinking

. . . she grew up knowing about AA since her mother was sober in AA but discovered her own need for alcohol, anyway.

They say AA ruins your drinking, and in my case, that was pretty much the truth. I come from a long line of alcoholics, and when I say alcoholics, I don't mean the happy, quiet drunks who pass out in front of the ball game on Sunday afternoon. The drunks in my family have traditionally been the angry, extremely non-functioning type of alcoholic. The kind who leave their toddlers home alone sleeping while they run out to the liquor store to stock up; and when they get pulled over for impaired driving, instead of handing over their documentation, they try to run the cop down and make a clean getaway. Both of my parents were alcoholics of this type, three out of four grandparents, and innumerable aunts, uncles, and cousins. In fact, I know of only two or three family members who don't have alcoholism, but they all seemed to marry people who throw knives at them during an argument. We're screwed up, all right.

My early childhood was unstable, to make an understatement. My father left when I was about two years old. He was just too drunk all the time to even try. My mother drank heavily and also fell into the habit of taking pills along with the booze, and would frequently have to call for an ambulance to take her to the hospital to pump her stomach. My sister and I would be taken to an emergency foster home on these nights, or sometimes our neighbor who lived in the attic apartment would take us in until my mother was discharged. This sort of thing lasted for two or three years, I suppose. I was about four years old at the time; my sister was five. I have vague memories of

25

people banging their fists on the door late at night, telling my sister and me it was okay to let them in, my mother drunk and crying on the floor in her bedroom. Sometimes these people were EMTs, sometimes they were AA members who were desperately trying to keep my mother alive, sometimes it was Child Welfare Services (we were pretty much on a first-name basis with them), or maybe sometimes it was all of them together. It's hard to remember.

Eventually, in the year I started kindergarten, my mother was sent off to a yearlong rehabilitation clinic. My father was now here to be found (which was probably for the best), so my sister and I were placed into foster care. We ended up living with a woman named Trudy, who had a teenaged daughter. I was unhappy in my foster home. The first thing Trudy did was to cut our hair short and keep it that way. How my mother cried when she saw that. The rehab staff spent the better part of that year trying to convince my mother to give us up for adoption, which she refused to do. When she was released, we went back to her, and except for one slip, she stayed sober by joining AA. In her first year of sobriety, she married another AA member, who couldn't stay sober. He had slip after slip after slip. I can remember the two of them fighting over a liquor bottle that she was trying to pour down the kitchen sink. Then one day my stepfather got drunk and cut his wrists and called the school to have my sister and me sent home to help him. We called my mother, and she came home from work, sent us up to a neighbor's apartment, and had an ambulance take him away. She filed for divorce, and we moved to a new town. I had just started second grade.

At that point, things became much more stable for us, though we were horribly poor. Even with food stamps, there were days when my mother searched her wardrobe for spare change to buy dinner, but she was sober and single, and things were better. She enrolled us in Ala-Tot and started taking us to meetings with her in the evenings, since we couldn't afford sitters. My sister and I would play in the church nurseries while my mother went to the meetings. We liked this. We liked the people, we liked sneaking up to the meeting to steal doughnuts off the coffee tables, we liked going to the diner afterwards. We even made a friend there, another little girl named Val, who was in the same boat as we were: Her mom was a single mother trying to get sober, with no babysitting funds. Val's mom was good friends with my mom, and we'd do cookouts, and sometimes sleepovers. Those were good days, in spite of the fact that my mother was always on the phone.

My mother's divorce took almost a year to be finalized. During that year, she fell in love with her divorce lawyer, another AA member who eventually divorced his own wife and moved in with us. Not long after that, we moved out of our little apartment in the projects to a country house on 12 acres in a wealthy town in northern New Jersey. I was 11 years old and had just started sixth grade. We got a couple of dogs and a horse, and all the nice things. My mother quit her job and began to look into starting her own business. But it wasn't so great in the country house. Mom started to drift away from AA, and so did her boyfriend, and before long they were both dry drunks and things got weird again. They fought all the time, sometimes physically. He cheated on her. She screamed at him and told us to pack our things, but she'd never really leave him. Also, even though they both didn't drink, they stocked a full bar for guests, something my mother hadn't done since she'd gotten sober. Two years after we moved there, I found my sister and her friends drinking right from those bottles after school one day. I'll never forget that: how scared I was, how sad. It was starting all over again, and there was nothing I could do about it. Since she'd gotten sober, my mother had been very open and direct with us about the disease of alcoholism. She bought us book after book to read and discuss with her, gave us AA literature in our Christmas stockings, and basically did everything she could to educate us, not just about the disease, but about the fact that we were at a high risk for developing it. She'd always say, "You'd never drink, would you, girls?" And we'd always say, "No! Never!" And back then, I really, really meant it. With every fiber of my heart and soul, I

27

never wanted to drink.

Until, of course, the summer after my freshman year of high school, when, not long after my mother had left the boyfriend and moved us into a different apartment, I found myself at a party that was in the process of breaking up because the cops were on the way. It was pandemonium in this kid's backyard, and someone running by with a six-pack of Moosehead beer said, "Hey, want one of these?"

"Sure," I said. I took the beer, opened it, and took a swallow. My entire childhood flashed through my head, and I just shrugged and drank, anyway.

And it was like nothing I'd ever tasted before. My liking for beer was instantaneous. I drank as much as I could before I had to leave to avoid the police, and I was furious with my mother for trying to keep this away from me. This was what I'd needed, just this.

From that day on, I drank whenever and wherever I could. And I drank to get drunk. There was never any other reason. Never. I preferred beer, but I'd drink just about anything. Within a year, I was out of control. Drinking was all I was interested in, and if I couldn't get anything to drink, I'd chain-smoke until I could. My grades dropped from A-B to C-D, and the occasional F. I changed my friends to make it easier to get to parties where there was alcohol. I experienced blackouts and hangovers and drank to the point of vomiting every weekend. Sometimes after vomiting, I'd be able to drink more, but most of the time I'd just pass out wherever I was, and people would have to wake me up, pump coffee into me, and try to get me into some type of normal state before I had to go home. Sometimes I would exhibit radical personality changes from drinking, and the kids I was with would get a little scared. Whenever this would happen, I would try to drink less at the next party so that they'd think I was normal. On these occasions, I'd slip a couple of cans of beer into my purse to take home with me. I'd drink them alone in my room, usually sitting in front of my mirror, crying.

The trouble with drinking to get drunk as a teenager is that your peers aren't taking you aside and saying things like, Hey, I've noticed you've been drinking quite a bit lately. Is everything okay? Do you need to talk about anything? Can I help? No, teenagers aren't saying that at all. What they're saying is more like, Wow! You're cool! and, Drink more! We all drank to get drunk. We played games designed to get us drunk as fast as possible: Quarters, Mexican, Thumper, Cardinal Puff . . . It was nonstop, and if you were drunk by midnight, no big deal. Everyone was. In the "cool" circles at my high school, it was just expected behavior.

But the problem was that most of the kids I was with weren't alcoholics. Their parents weren't, either, and so drinking and getting a little tipsy for them was just a lark, something that could be laughed off and forgotten as just another dumb thing we all did in high school. These kids could drink to get a little drunk, just a little, and then go home, dash upstairs, and brush their teeth before kissing their parents goodnight and wake up feeling reasonably well and ready for the day. I didn't drink like that, and my experiences of being drunk were more difficult and intense. I seemed to be the only one who blacked out, who had the occasional evening of hysterics, and who hid beer in my purse for later just in case I couldn't get any more. I was always so concerned about the next drink. No one else seemed to be.

In addition, coming home to my house after a night of drinking was a completely different experience. There was no lighthearted, *Oh, well, kids will be kids* attitude at my house. At my house, my mother, who had over 10 years of sobriety under her belt, would meet you at the door with a Big Book and a breathalyzer kit, and you'd be drilled, question after question after question: Did you drink? Who was there? Is that smoke I smell? What's in your purse? And on and on and on, until you were about ready to pass out right there on the floor.

Trying to launch a huge alcoholic drinking career at the age of 15 when your mom's in AA and has been dragging you to meetings since you were about eight years old is enormously difficult. I had started drinking in the hopes that I would be the one rare family member who wasn't an alcoholic, but within a year or so, I knew I was one. I would never have admitted it to anyone, but deep inside I knew. I remembered what I'd overheard in all those meetings, and the meetings after the meetings, and all the pamphlets I'd read while waiting for my mother to finish her coffee and stop talking to everyone so we could go home. The "44 Questions" had become more like a checklist for me. I'd mentally check each one off as I experienced them: memory loss, change in personality, hangovers, drinking alone, drinking in the morning. By my senior year, I'd hit most, if not all, of them. But I still never admitted it to myself or anyone else, until one night when my boyfriend was walking me home from a party where I'd been drunker than usual and had had one of those Jekyll-and-Hyde personality changes. I imagine now how afraid he must have been to be taking me home in that condition. I remarked that Thomas and his friends must think I'm really crazy, and my boyfriend immediately responded with, "No, they don't think you're crazy. They just think you're an alcoholic, that's all." He was so matter of fact about it that I realized that he thought so, too, that probably everyone thought it, and that they were right. I almost—almost—said, "Well, of course I'm an alcoholic!" but at the last second, I didn't. To admit it would mean I'd have to do something about it, and I certainly wasn't ready for that. I learned something valuable that night, though. I learned that I wasn't fooling anyone.

After that, I tried to tone my drinking down a little bit. My mother had started grounding me for drinking, and there was one whole semester in my senior year when I wasn't allowed to go out at all. With nothing else to do, and knowing it would get me to college, I had picked up my schoolwork again and finished high school with high marks. I was accepted at Boston University and went off to school there for a year after high school, knowing we couldn't afford it but believing my mother when she said she'd find a way to pay for it. I spent most of that first year of college drinking. It was freeing, being able to drink in my dorm room, going out to bars or to parties, not having to do battle with my sober mother at the end of the night. But it didn't last. My grades weren't too bad, but my mother had stopped paying the tuition bill halfway through the year and then transferred the bill into my name, and I had to withdraw from the university that summer because you aren't eligible for financial aid if you owe the college money. I stayed in Boston as long as I could, but, in the end, I had to go back home. I owed the university roughly $6,000, had no real job and no real friends, my boyfriend had broken up with me because he'd met someone else, and I had no idea what to do with my life. I went back to New Jersey in the fall, moved back in with my mother, and got a job taking care of horses. Everyone I knew was in college either full time or part time, had definite plans and career goals, and were steadily working toward those goals. I had no idea what I wanted to do, other than drink as much as possible. I couldn't apply to any schools because the university wouldn't release my transcripts because I owed them money. Never had I felt so stuck in my life.

For most of that winter, I just worked in the barn, fought with my mother, and slept. I didn't have any friends in town, so I didn't have anyone to drink with or to buy me liquor. Eventually, I ran into some old high school friends and started going out with them, but the drinking had changed. They weren't drinking like we used to. They were drinking like normal adults, and I didn't know how to do that. My drinking problem was becoming more noticeable to them and to me. My mother had also been going through some changes, and they weren't for the better. She'd been on her dry drunk for quite a few years and had begun to exhibit strange, paranoid behavior and was full of rage and hostility toward me. As for me, I was furious with her for how she'd handled the Boston University bill. We didn't get along, but I needed to live there while I figured out how to pay off the debt she'd handed to me; and since deep inside she knew what she'd done was wrong, she knew better than to charge me rent or kick me out. It was an awful, awful year. I got out and away from her to drink when I could, but even that had become less enjoyable. Nothing was working anymore. At the age of 20, I felt that my life simply wasn't worth living.

Just before Independence Day that summer, I was sitting on the back porch, having my morning coffee and cigarettes, mulling over my situation. I knew I was an alcoholic, and I think I was sitting there trying to resign myself to a life like my mother's was before she got sober. I was telling myself that I'd better not marry or have kids because I knew I was going to be the same kind of drunk as she'd been, and trying to figure out what kind of job I should get so that I didn't cause too much harm from my drinking. So there I sat, downsizing my life to accommodate my drinking, when, out of nowhere, a thought that didn't seem to be my own popped into my head: You know, you could quit drinking now.

My eyes widened at the possibility. Quit now? Now? At this age? Hell, I wasn't even 21 years old yet! No one quits before they're 21, right? I hadn't even had the chance to walk into a bar and order a drink legally yet. How in the world could I just quit? You could join AA.

I sat there all morning, drinking coffee, and just letting the possibility of giving up drinking sink in. It had never occurred to me that I could join AA at such a young age, but the more I thought about it, the more I realized that this was something that might work. AA had always been something that belonged to my mother. It had saved her life way back when, and I knew all about it, but I'd never really thought I'd join. Eventually, I got up and went back inside. My mother and I had had an argument the night before and were barely speaking to each other. She looked at me as I came in and asked if I'd thought anything over, or something like that. I don't remember what the fight had been about or what I was supposed to be thinking over, but I remember I looked at her and said, "I think I'm going to quit drinking." She rose and went to the kitchen without a word, dug through a drawer, and found me a meeting guide. She flipped to Saturday and scanned the list and then tapped the page and said,

"Try that one."

It was a Saturday morning women's meeting. I'd like to tell you that I joined AA, got a sponsor, did the steps, and lived happily ever after, but it didn't really happen that way. I walked through the door, and someone asked if I was new, and I said, "Not really. I've been coming to meetings since I was a kid." Then I went and sat down and didn't talk to anyone. I didn't drink anymore, but I didn't really get involved in AA or open up to anyone for a few months. It was easy to go along as if I had lots of time. I knew the literature, I knew the preamble, and I could recite "How It Works" or the "12 Steps" or the "Traditions." It was easy to act like an old timer, except for the fact that I was only 20 years old. It was a silly way to start, and eventually loneliness and resentment led me to being more honest about why I was there. When I finally confessed to everyone that I was a newcomer in spite of the fact that I knew everything there was to know about AA, they all laughed, assigned me a sponsor, gave me a phone list, and made me celebrate my 90 days, which I'd hidden from everyone. So five months after I took my last drink, on the day before I turned 21 years old (and my birthday is on New Year's Eve!), I stood up in front of all these women and accepted a 90-Day pin.

My sponsor suggested that I begin to branch out and try lots of other meetings. She said that there were a lot of meetings in the area that young people my age attended and that I should find them and spend time with them. So, after a while, I did what she said. I found a Thursday night meeting near my house, and when I walked through the door, the first person I saw was an old high school drinking buddy of mine. She looked at me and cheered, "You made it!" and then she ran over and hugged me. It turned out that half a dozen people at that meeting were old high school drinking buddies. It was surreal. So, slowly I started building up a schedule of meetings that I went to regularly. I found another sponsor and started working on the steps. I got a new job as an office assistant. I called Boston University's Claims Department and asked to set up a payment schedule for the $6,000 I owed them. They were quite agreeable about this, and even said that, since I was setting up a plan with them, they would release one copy of my transcript. I used that single transcript to apply to Rutgers University for the following year. That gave me a year to finish paying off Boston. If all went well, I could be going back to college in another year, debt free. And I kept going to meetings. I picked up a coffee-making commitment for an enormous Saturday night speakers meeting in Chester and found that I enjoyed service work. I liked being the first one to the meeting, making all the coffee, setting out the cups, the cream and sugar. Even washing the urns out afterward was fun because so many people came in to help.

But secretly, I kept myself a bit distant. I couldn't give myself 100 percent to AA yet. Because I was going back to college, you see. And I knew, deep in my heart I just knew, that I would drink again as soon as I got back into the dorms. Then, one night, a new person showed up at my regular step meeting. She had come to visit a friend who was a regular at that meeting, but there was something so familiar about her that finally I asked her if I knew her. It was Val, my friend from long ago when we used to go to meetings with our moms. She'd been in recovery for a couple of years and was a junior at Rutgers. I told her that I'd been accepted at Rutgers for the following year. Then I told her I was really afraid that I'd drink again as soon as I moved on campus. And that's when she told me about Recovery Housing. Apparently, there was some enormous assistance program for students in recovery at Rutgers: therapy, group therapy, meetings and on-campus housing just for people in recovery. I couldn't believe it. Val was in this program and lived in this housing! Amazing! She wrote down a phone number for the director of the Rutgers University recovery program, gave me a hug, and left.

I called first thing Monday morning, and just like that, I was connected to a recovering community even before I got to the school. This saved my life. I now knew I could go to college and stay sober. I finally managed to get my other foot in AA's door and keep it there. The four years at Rutgers were a gift. I participated in the group therapy sessions and the private therapy sessions and went to meetings all over town. I lived in an on-campus apartment with three other women in sobriety, and there were more recovery people in the surrounding apartments. If you started to feel freaked out about something, or had to deal with sudden cravings for beer, all you had to do was go sit in your living room or poke your head out into the hallway and someone was there to talk to. I discovered who I am and the things I like. I became a straight-A student. I made life-long friends and met the man I would eventually marry, and we're still sober and married today. Those four years had their crazy moments, to be sure, but, for the most part, I think they were the best years of my life. I'd been sober a little over a year when I got to Rutgers, and right after I graduated, I celebrated five years of sobriety. I had been immersed in a sober world for four straight years, and I'm certain that those years are the reason I'm still sober today.

Right after graduation, my husband and I moved west to Colorado, where we married and had our children. We're still in Colorado today, but we come back to New Jersey to see family, and always if there's a Recovery Housing reunion. We never miss those. I've been sober over 15 years now, and I live a pretty normal life. This is something I never expected to have: a nice, simple, normal life. A lot of things have happened in the past 15 years, and not all of it has been wonderful. We've had hard times as well as good, but there's never been a moment that I thought drinking was an option or a solution for any problem or difficult event in my life.

To a certain extent, as much as possible after so much water under the bridge, my family relationships have improved. My father eventually died of cancer and late-stage alcoholism. After a lifetime of drinking, smoking, and living in his car, he eventually came home to us to die. He stopped drinking in his last year because the doctors told him another drink would kill him within an hour, and not long after that he was diagnosed with stomach and liver cancer and released into hospice care. My sister took him in, and he spent his last days on her living room couch. I was 30 years old, pregnant with my first daughter, and I flew in late on a Friday night to see him. He was awake and alert as I'd never seen him before, even though he couldn't talk anymore. His eyes sparkled at me, and we held hands, and I realized that I was seeing him sober for the very first time. He died the next afternoon while my mother and my sister and I were eating Chinese food in the basement.

My mother finally drifted back into AA and ended her long dry drunk. She has something like 30 years of sobriety at this point. She's a regular old old-timer now and still goes to meetings. She never married again, still runs her own business, and is living a relatively happy life. For someone who had numerous near-death experiences at the end of her own drinking, she's made a miraculous recovery. Even though our relationship is still strained in many ways, she's my mom, and I love her a lot. As for me, I have two daughters of my own now, one preschooler and one toddler. I stopped working a year ago to stay home with them, so my days are pretty hectic. I still struggle with anger and feelings of rage, and I have days where I'm convinced my kids will need years of therapy just because I'm the one raising them. But they've never known me drunk, never had Child Welfare Services banging on the door in the middle of the night, and don't have parents who fight like drunken cats and dogs all the time. At some point, I'll start dragging them to meetings and slipping AA literature into their Christmas stockings. I think it will be good for them. They're at a high risk for developing this disease themselves, and if I teach them about it like my mom taught me, maybe they'll quit young, too, if they have a problem. Because as I said at the beginning, AA ruins your drinking. Thank God for that.

Chapter 4

Not the Smoothest Guy on Campus

. . . he was lonely and drank to feel better. Not the coolest guy
when he drank; at 19, he decided to stop and found recovery.

Drinking was it. It fixed everything. I was no longer afraid, and I no longer hurt. It was hard to think that, at the age of 12, a person could feel so utterly awful. Most the time I was at home, I lived in fear and ridicule of my father. Most the time I spent outside the house, I spent in fear of other people.

I never was good around other people. I always knew I wanted to be around people and have friends, but I was just never good at it. Even the people who I thought were a bit odd thought I was strange. Finding pleasure in the simple things that kids did was not enough for me. As I can see now, the need to kill the pain that I was living with always required a little more excitement. I never could understand the point of doing things like homework or listening to the teacher. It just didn't make sense. Looking out the window wishing I was on the playground always seemed more appealing than actually being present mentally. This was the start of my pattern for tuning out.

The teachers needed a way to keep me out of their hair. Their fix was to put me in harder classes. I was even placed in a "Learning Unlimited" group. Here I was, in a group of really smart kids, thinking, "I'm not this smart; why am I here?" Story of my life. I never felt good enough or smart enough, although I always secretly hoped that I was. Of course, this did not fix my behavioral problems. All this did was add to my frustration that I actually had to pay attention to get by again.

There were a few things along the way that did fill up some

of my time before alcohol became my distraction of choice: girls and guitars. The latter became a passion for me that I also thought was the answer to my emptiness. As you could probably imagine, my self-centeredness (of which I was not aware at that time) precluded any chance of a good relationship. They pretty much all ended in pain on both sides of the fence. I could barely tolerate being alone, yet, often, that was what I was. At the end of my drinking, it was that loneliness that made me seek help. In the last days of my drinking, at the ripe old age of 19, I had very few friends and no girlfriend and no way to go home to regroup and try again.

My second year at Rutgers is where my drinking ended and my sober life started. Really, I was quite torn. I wanted to leave college altogether. My grades were lousy, and my idea of getting an electrical engineering degree was on its way out. I did not have the guts to quit. I really wanted to be in a band and play music. I did not care what I did for money. That was not going to happen. I told my mom I was quitting, and her reaction to that made me stay in school—still a sore spot in my sobriety.

That first semester of my second year, my girlfriend of four years was gone, my friends were all back home, and my folks had moved again. I was lost. All I wanted was a new girlfriend and to get drunk. Whenever I could get alcohol, I would drink. I always drank to get drunk. The weekends were always spent around the frat houses. Really, all I was doing was medicating the pain I was in. At a certain point, the alcohol had stopped taking away the pain and started to make things worse. The last year of my drinking, I was a blackout drinker. It wasn't until people started telling me how funny I was the night before that I realized I did not remember what I did the night before.

The last drunk I had before trying to get help I was in a gray out. I kind of remember what happened. It started out with my drinking by myself and then deciding to do some laundry. Downstairs in the laundromat was a girl who I was friends with and liked. From what I remember, I pulled one of the classic drunk "I love you" routines in front of the washer, dryer, and a few of her friends. Not the smoothest guy on campus, I can assure you. I had made a few attempts at this point to limit how much I drank when I drank, with little to no success. The next morning, I asked God to help me. This last humiliating and painful episode of drinking was my final straw. From the phone book, I got the number for AA and made my first call. They said there was a meeting at Mine Street right on the Rutgers Campus. That was October 14, 1988. My continuous sobriety did not start until January 1, 1989, just a little more than two months later.

I'm not sure whether I would have been able to stay sober outside of sober housing. It wasn't just the housing; it was the Rutgers University recovery program people, the group. AA kept me sober, and the on-campus group and the sober housing community kept me going to AA. I was exactly where I needed to be in order to get and stay sober. I don't think it was a coincidence. The Mine Street meeting was great if you were a student. It was full of people who had gone through what I was going through, trying get sober and obtain a degree at the same time. There were lots of young people, people my age, which really helped. I had been so isolated the last year of my drinking that to be around people was wonderful. But I was still in pain.

I found my sponsor at Mine Street; well, actually, he found me. One night when I thought I would go out drinking, I shared at the meeting that I was going out drinking tonight unless someone might be able to talk me out of it. *Voila*, instant sponsor. The guy sitting next to me, who had about five years sober at the time, said, "I am your new sponsor, and we are going to a meeting tomorrow morning, so don't be hung over."

I was still in pain. Now the depression started to set in, but I stayed sober. They gave me a nickname: "psycho gyro." Long story, not important. The point is that I had people around me who liked me. Sober housing was the place to be: lots of coffee, nicotine, and meetings. It was hard not to go to meetings. There were the set meetings that almost everyone went to: Monday night Cook, Tuesday night Sand Hill, Friday Mine

Street, Sunday at Robert Wood Johnson, and, of course, the on-campus recovery program group.

I would go to these meetings and carpool. We would go out after the meetings for coffee. There was the Manville dance and the Cook dance. There were any number of things to do and places to go, so I didn't have to isolate. All the while, we were all focused on not going back out. Some of us did and never made it back. In the La La Land Utopia of the sober housing group, it was a very powerful reminder that what we were being given at that time was a chance to live.

I felt alive. Heck, I felt everything. Now this was both a blessing and a curse. What is really clear in my memory now is a turning point in my life that happened to me at the Cook Monday night meeting. As you walked in the front door, there was always a big crowd of people who were smoking and talking. It was hard to get through without at least a couple of how are yous or hugs. I ran into my sponsor, and, of course, I was there with the whole gaggle from housing. There were a lot of people there, too, who were not from housing or the college, many of whom I was friends with. After all the hellos and heys and hugs and good to see yous, a very strange sensation came over me: I was happy. Not the drunk or high kind of happy; just an overwhelming feeling of being cared for and truly liked. I was no longer in so much pain.

Of course, sobriety and life are not that easy. It was not pure bliss 100 percent of the time. As a matter of fact, it got hard. The point is, now I had enough relief from where I had been when I first came into the rooms to make it through the hard stuff without drinking.

AA and my friends in sober housing were good. They were good for me, but I had more help, help with the scary stuff. Andrea was my primary counselor. Some stuff can't be worked on in the spotlight of an AA meeting. I still thought I was stupid and unlovable or even unlikable. My family dynamics had set me up for a certain way of dealing with people and situations in my life that was not in the best interest of my peace of mind and long-term serenity. I had things that I had done that I was ashamed of and did not want to tell anyone. I knew for sure that I was what I feared the most: flawed. Then the next major life-changing experience happened. I opened up to Andrea and told her who I was and what I had done. Surprisingly enough, she did not throw me out of her office. She set me straight on my twisted view of myself. I was no longer a pariah in my own mind. All of the counselors I dealt with at the Rutgers University recovery program were fantastic. They saved my life.

I met my wife in sober housing. We have been married 10 years, all sober. We did follow the unwritten two-years-before-a- relationship rule, kind of. It is amazing all the wonderful things that I received that came out of being in sober housing.

My second sponsor, who was also an on-campus recovery group member at one time, also had a huge impact on my life. He was the one with whom I did my fifth step. My life changed not too long after doing my fifth step. It was then that the craving to drink finally started to leave me. Here is a man who listened to my scary stuff without judgment, only compassion. He shared his home with me when I needed to get out of living with my parents. He let me borrow a large sum of money when I lost my job. He listened to me. It was his example of how to be a man, a responsible caring man who shaped the man I try to be today.

That is what still overwhelms me. I could not comprehend the amount of caring that was so freely given from so many in that small community that revolves around one woman. And that is what I aspire to be, although sometimes with little success.

I am not perfect; my self-centeredness still looms large over who I am. I still have fears and do battle with being depressed and angry. My relationships with others are hit and miss, and very often I choose to just isolate, but I stay sober. I know it's up to me to grow, and I do. Sometimes it takes a long time, and God has been very patient with me. But it is always my intention to defer to His better judgment and keep trying to improve.

Working the steps is an integral part of my life. It defines how I grow and how I leave behind my way former way, my drinking way of dealing with the world. Small steps—sometimes it's small steps toward getting better. I have been sober for quite some time, and I never take that for granted. There have been other areas of my life where I have been powerless to control my behavior. This is an awesome reminder that I am just one drink away from my next drunk.

My life is good. My life is good because people, wonderful people, gave without asking for anything in return. It is my hope that I may one day be able to do the same.

Chapter 5

The First Drink

*. . . he did well enough in school to get into law school before his
alcoholism caught up with him and turned his life upside down.*

My mother was raised Christian Scientist, and my father
was raised Catholic. They had met in college and had both left
their respective churches, dissatisfied with their dogma. My
father was German/Irish and came from a poor neighborhood in
Pittsburgh, where the men worked in the steel mills. It was a
hard-drinking culture. My mother's family had never allowed
alcohol in the house, so my mother had her hands full with a
husband who drank every day and who went out with his
coworkers every Friday, sometimes not arriving home until
Saturday morning.

My earliest memories are of my mother's frantically
pacing around the house when my father did not come home.
She shared her worst fears with us, striking fear in our hearts.
When I was older, say six or seven, I would be sent to march
into the bar where my father was and ask him to come home.
This would enrage him and invite ridicule from his colleagues,
whom I despised. My mother would clutch me in her arms
afterward and get me to promise over and over that I would
never drink like Daddy.

Then there were the trips to Pittsburgh to see my
relatives. My father would drink until 4 or 5 a.m. at his brother's
or sister's house, and then insist on driving us back to our
grandparents' house, across town. My mother never learned to
drive a car, even though we lived in the suburbs and even though
my father was often too incapacitated to drive. Those were the

most terrifying nights; one night our car went over an embankment and several feet down into a ditch. Miraculously, no one was hurt. Another night, we went through the Liberty Tubes in Pittsburgh, a tunnel through a mountain, going the wrong way. I remember seeing the headlights coming toward us and thinking I was going to die . . . but I didn't.

I play the flute now and love music, and loved it just as much when I was five years old and played the triangle in the Christmas show at school. It was the most exciting thing I had ever done, and I was so eager for mommy and daddy to see me. They didn't. My father went out drinking before the Christmas break with his colleagues, and as I said, my mother did not drive. I can still feel the pain and rage of that night, 41 years later.

When I was 12, I worked for the stage crew of my school play. I was invited to the cast party. I went to an all-male, private school on a scholarship. So I was in a mansion with all the older kids and the pretty girls, and it was so exciting. Then my best friend invited me down to the basement. That was where the wine was. Even though I had always promised my mother that I would not drink, I did not hesitate. I filled a coca-cola glass with red wine. It tasted terrible. But after a few sips, it felt so wonderful. All of my fears, my worries went away, and I felt euphoria! Donny went upstairs, but I stayed downstairs with the wine. I drank until I couldn't drink more. I was drunk for the first time.

Thereafter, I went to parties like that every weekend, sometimes two or more. The kids I went to school with were wealthy and lived in big homes, and their parents were often away. Keg parties were the focus of my week. During the week, I was on track to be the valedictorian at my high school, the good kid, but on the weekends, I hung out with the cool crowd. I began to smoke marijuana soon thereafter and took other drugs if offered, like Quaaludes, speed, mescaline, and LSD. I fancied myself part of the counter culture. My heroes were Jefferson Airplane, The Grateful Dead, The Beatles, The Doors, and Led Zeppelin.

Blackouts started in high school. I woke up several times on various neighbors' lawns, several houses from where I lived. I guess I had been afraid to go in the night before. My parents punished, me but nothing worked. When grounded, I just smoked pot in my room and listened to records.

My first great setback, at least to my mind, was that I did not get accepted into Princeton. I went instead to Rutgers on a full- caddy scholarship, bitter at the unknown forces that had blocked my path to the Ivy League school I dreamed of. However, college meant not living at home, and I was thrilled. I went to every fraternity rush party, three a night, six days a week, for three weeks. The fact that I was 17 and the drinking age was 18 was no obstacle. I never joined or even pledged a fraternity; I just liked the rush parties. I liked them so much that I developed mononucleosis my first few weeks in college. The doctor at Rutgers Health Services told me that I could not drink for 90 days or it would damage my liver. For the first time since I was 12, I tried to stop drinking. This lasted for 50-plus days. Then I had tickets to see a Sparks concert at the Capitol Theater and, while in the audience, was passed a joint laced with angel dust. I couldn't resist, and I was back on a tear again. I wouldn't be able to stop drinking again until I went to AA.

I met a girl in my sophomore year who lived in my dorm. She was a nice Jewish girl from a good neighborhood in East Brunswick. She and I fell in love and were together for close to the rest of my college years. But she had never seen drinking like mine before. She thought it was just a college phase and tolerated it—until my senior year, when it became unbearable. When she broke up with me, it shocked me. I asked her, "Why are you leaving me?" She said, "I know you love me, but I am not your first love. Your first love is booze. I think you have a sickness, and I hope you get better. But I cannot get you better, so I must leave." Little did I know how prophetic her words were. At the time, all I could do was feel sorry for myself.

I got through college not as the straight A student I was in high school but, rather, as an A-, B+ of the party boy. It was in college that I began to have run-ins with the law. The first time was down at the shore, while smoking pot in my friend's car in the parking lot of a beachside nightclub. The police arrested us for the possession of some marijuana cigarettes. When the police asked to look in the trunk, my friend told them that he had lost the trunk key weeks ago and would the police be able to open it for him? The police scoffed saying, do we look like your personal locksmith? My friend was a good actor, for if the police had opened that trunk and found his stash, our lives would have been ruined. Then there was the inevitable drunk driving, again coming home from, as we say in New Jersey, "the shore." I had drunk over a quart of vodka at my friend's house. They begged me to stay over. I refused and drove home in a blackout. My next memory is of the police asking me to say the alphabet. The first arrest was dismissed under a program for first offenders of minor offenses. The second arrest for drunk driving resulted in a 60-day license suspension and attendance at four educational classes, where I was given a test about my drinking habits. I realized that, if I answered the questions honestly, I might have to do something drastic, like go to AA meetings, so I lied. They classified me as a social drinker, and I was happy with that. I was free to take my drinking into my next stage of life as a college graduate.

I graduated without any job prospects. I kept working at the local bank as a teller and at the local sub shop, Little Teddy's, which supplied me with my entire week's worth of food. But those jobs were not to last. I was fired from Little Teddy's for not showing up on Labor Day weekend because I was tripping down in Belmar. I was fired from the bank job after not showing up as the early drive-in teller at 8:30 one morning due to a hangover. When I saw the line of cars honking their horns at the bank as I rode up on my bicycle, I knew I was in trouble.

So I took my Rutgers BA and went back to the

Plainfield Country Club to be a caddy, where I had worked in high school. Among the adult caddies, mostly grizzled long-time alcoholics, I felt strangely at home. Then one day, I was caddying for the father of a guy I knew from high school. He knew that I had been the valedictorian at Wardlaw and had attended Rutgers on a scholarship from the Plainfield Country Club, so he was shocked to see me holding his golf bags. He told me to report to his office the next morning. He owned a mortgage company, and I was given a job as a collector.

There I met Donna. She was 10 years older than me and lonely. She took me in like an abandoned puppy. I lived with her without paying rent, and she took care of me in many ways, even though the relationship was no more than platonic. After six months, she decided I should go to law school, as that is what I always told people I had wanted to do. So she signed me up for the LSAT test, which I took slightly hungover, and then she typed, at my dictation, six law school applications. I was accepted, miraculously, by five out of six, and chose Rutgers Law School in Camden.

I moved to Camden and saw this as my chance to start over. I was ready for a geographical cure. All I needed to do was to change people, places, and things, which worked for a little while. I made the Dean's list the first semester. I went to the local pub, The Grill, for lunch and would have only one or two beers before going back to class. But at the end of the semester, there were a spate of parties. When my roommate found me the morning after sleeping in the bushes next to our Ferry Station apartment, he began to worry about me. Next semester, my Grill lunches became more extended. By the second year, I was a straight-C student, and my drinking was back to being not only a daily problem, but an around-the-clock phenomenon. By the first semester of the third year, I had stopped going to classes altogether.

I woke up each morning and smoked pot to quiet my stomach and calm the shakes so I did not get sick. Then I would drink what was left over from the night before, if anything, and go to the first liquor store of the day for supplies. I went for liquor three times a day, each time at a different store, to hide from the liquor store clerks how much I was buying. I watched television all day, old reruns of Bewitched, I Dream of Jeannie, etc. I had stopped going to class altogether. I lived in a house with two roommates. One was a heroin addict, who nodded out on the couch all day. The other was an artist, who was a speed freak. He would get wired up, crank up his chainsaw, and hack away at tree trunks in the back yard, thus creating his art. His girlfriend was the DJ at the Grill. One night when he had made her angry, she came home with me to get back at him. I acquiesced, with no second thoughts about the chain saw.

This house of cards collapsed when finals came. I reported for my Wills, Estates, and Trusts exam without having bought the book. I sat in the room with my fellow students and wrote my identification number, and then was stumped. The proctor for the exam, a secretary from the administration offices who also haunted the grill and with whom I had slept in the past, took pity on me and told me I could take the final in her office upstairs. When that didn't work, she suggested that I get a six-pack at the Grill to calm my shakes. I thought that was a good idea and got a six-pack of 16-ounce Schmidt's. But no inspiration came, and I handed in the blank piece of paper.

When I told the Dean's secretary, whom I also knew from the Grill, what had happened, she was very cold and told me that, with one "F," I would be expelled from law school. I was surprised by her cold reaction until much later, when I learned she was in Al-Anon. She was just being careful not to enable someone she saw who was hitting bottom.

With that news, my only recourse was to plead insanity. So I proceeded to the health center and made an appointment with the psychiatrist. But he was too tricky for me. He said right out that I was an alcoholic and that he was referring me to the director of the university recovery program for intervention. I told him that he had gotten it wrong and that all I needed was individual counseling. He ignored me and got the director on the phone while I spouted off bad language in the background. The director jumped into to her Saab and came down to see me in Camden.

She was very crafty. She didn't talk to me about me. She talked to me about my alcoholic father, my grandmother who was a bag lady on the streets of Pittsburgh, and my uncle who died of cirrhosis at the ripe old age of 28. She got me to promise to go to rehab right after New Year's (as I protested that I could not be in rehab on Christmas, my birthday, and on New Year's!). I promised to go to an AA meeting. In exchange, she would, by powers vested in her by the provost under a brand-new program called the Student Assistance Program, allow me to receive "T" grades for my courses. Then, if I agreed to take classes for one extra semester and made up the "T" grades, I would be allowed to receive my JD. Today, such an offer seems like a no-brainer, but then I told the recovery program director I would "consider it," as if I were doing HER a favor.

I took no more finals that semester. I had promised to go to an AA meeting, but I made no effort to go. Finally, Donna called me to ask about my meeting, and when she found out I hadn't gone, she drove down from North Plainfield, New Jersey, to Camden to drive me three miles to my first meeting in Audubon. I thought it was a dreary, dismal crowd of people. I was horrified. They gave me the yellow book about how to stop drinking one day at a time. I went home that night, bought a quart of vodka, and started to read. It made sense, until I passed out in a stupor.

Christmas was terrible. I was too hung over to enjoy it. On my birthday, Donna and I went to see American Buffalo with Al Pacino on Broadway. I wish I could remember it. Before the show, we had visited my old roommate from college, and he had slipped me two hits of acid for my birthday, and I took them both. When Donna said she would take me anywhere for my birthday dinner, I chose Nathan's on Times Square.

New Year's Eve was terrible because I tried not to drink.

I smoked pot instead. The next day, there was so much booze left over at my friends' house (I guess because I hadn't drunk), they invited me over to finish it off. Although that was the day I was supposed to check into rehab, I went and got drunk. The next day, the recovery program director was calling, bugging me about breaking my promise to go to rehab, so I bought a pint of vodka, drank it, and went to Perth Amboy General Hospital Center for Living. They had a 21-day program. Because I had no insurance, a 28-day program was not offered.

When I got there, I felt such a sense of relief. It was like a ten-ton weight was taken off my shoulders. Suddenly, I didn't have to manage this problem. Others wanted to manage it for me, and I was glad to give it to them. I can't describe how this occurred, but there was something powerful about being in a room full of people who understood, both patients and caregivers, who were all in the same club. I loved going to the AA meetings in the hospital and read the Big Book with relish. I developed an appetite for food for the first time in a long time and began to feel my body healing. I was happy and had hope for the first time in a long time. They told me that I shouldn't return to the house with the heroin addict and the speed freak. And then, out of the blue, I got a call from a good friend at school. She said I could live at her house, right across the street from campus. When asked how I could pay the rent, she said she would get me a job as a bail interviewer with her at the Philadelphia Municipal Court. I was amazed how differently my life was going after being exposed to the program for a matter of days.

I moved back to Camden, already a week late for the next semester of classes. I went to a meeting the first day and felt resentment when nobody called upon me. I came home, went under the Ben Franklin Bridge to the corner of 5th and Vine, and stuck my $5 bill through the crack in the wall to get my nickel bag of pot. I went home and started smoking. Then the recovery program director called and asked how I was doing. She was glad I went to my first meeting and appalled at what I had done thereafter. She told me to flush it down the toilet and call Intergroup immediately. I didn't flush it down the toilet until two months later, but I never touched it again and called Intergroup immediately. The person who answered was also named George, and this made me feel good. He sent a guy named Bruce to meet me, and Bruce took me back to that meeting in Audubon I had disliked so much—except this time, the meeting looked bright and cheerful and full of laughter. People listened to me but gave me no sympathy for my bad behavior. For someone who craves acceptance, I knew that I would get a much better reaction when I could come in and say I stayed sober for 24 hours. So that is just what I did the next day, and the day after, and the day after that. Bruce became my sponsor, and George became a friend. I read the "12 Steps and the 12 Traditions," and I worked each step with Bruce until I understood it and thought I could live it. I went to 120 meetings in 90 days and got my 90-day pin, of which I was very proud.

Because I was a law student, I had also called an organization, independent of AA, called Lawyers Concerned for Lawyers. This group had an AA-type meeting just for lawyers and law students, where they could discuss issues that arose from a profession where one is always under the scrutiny of the bar with regard to one's behavior. I loved the counsel and support from these busy and successful attorneys. They gave me the confidence to finish law school and to pass the bar in two states.

My grades for my last semester of law school were A, A, A, A, and A+. I got a letter from the Dean, expressing, quite frankly, shock and surprise. But I was ready to take the bar exam, which I passed with flying colors. However, when it came time to be admitted to the bar, the Committee on Character and Fitness called to advise me that my application had been deferred, subject to a hearing on my moral character due to my status as a recovering alcoholic. I was told that my arrest record was no bar, as I had fully disclosed it. I was full of rage and self-pity but had no time for that, as my lawyers' group rallied around me and one attorney stepped forward to represent me. He obtained the head of the Impaired Physicians group as an expert witness on my behalf. He requested the head of the Philadelphia LCL group to be a fact and character witness. My hearing went without a hitch, although I think the bar examiners would have been shocked if they had known that my defense team and witnesses, a very distinguished and well-known group, were all recovering alcoholics and/or drug addicts!

So I was admitted to the bars of New Jersey and New York and learned how to be in a helping profession while learning to help myself and others by going to meetings daily. I loved going to meetings and meeting people from all over the state and in other places when I went on vacation. While I waited to try my first case, in the courthouse in Newark, I was very comforted when I looked around and saw four very well-regarded attorneys nearby, ready to help me and give me confidence, all of whom were in the program and all by happenstance. Such was the way of the program.

Day by day, month by month, time passed, and it became easier and easier to live without alcohol and drugs. I lost 50 pounds and finally, two years after I stopped drinking, realized that women were interested in me again. I learned all over again how to date. I joined the state and national bar associations and worked with other recovering lawyers to develop model guidelines for lawyer assistance programs throughout the state and country. I was asked to sit on the first board of trustees of the New Jersey Lawyers Assistance Program and was on the founding board of trustees for a halfway house for recovering women and their children in Long Branch, New Jersey.

I started out working at a tiny law firm in Jersey City. When a friend left a bigger firm in New Brunswick, I got the job and doubled my salary in one year. After two years, a headhunter was referred to me and got me an interview at the third largest firm in New Jersey. I got the job and tripled my salary. I was amazed at how things worked when I applied my energies to work and health instead of to alcohol.

I worked at that firm for eight more years but was nagged by the desire to get away from law and work in finance. I wanted to get an MBA. So I left the firm and went to work for AIG, who sponsored me to get an MBA at night at New York University. Within five years, I had left the practice of law and had become a financial analyst. I now work at a well-known firm on Wall Street.

As I look back on my 21 years in AA, all of the things I thought were impossible to accomplish became eminently doable in sobriety. More than improving my work product, sobriety allowed me to become more in touch with other human beings. I became better able at communicating with others because I was more in touch with my own issues and feelings and, thus, better able to be in touch with theirs. I became more empathetic.

Sobriety has given me a better spiritual life. Learning to live one day at a time takes daily practice but has many rewards. The raging feelings of my youth have been calmed as I have finally begun to mature as a person.

My capacity for love has increased, along with my capacity for acceptance and tolerance of the sickness and shortcomings of others. This is still a challenge when dealing with my family. I have a lot to learn about loving them with detachment. I am blessed with a considerable amount of friends but still wrestle with the issues of being a controlling person.

I have not yet been able to make that leap of faith that one takes in marrying and starting a family, and I may be running out of time. But there is a wonderful woman in my life who may yet show me that path.

I am so grateful for my friends in AA, not only in New York City where I live, but all over New Jersey and Philadelphia, and in London, Amsterdam, Paris, Tokyo, Madrid, Dublin, San Francisco, Seattle, Cleveland, Jacksonville, New Orleans, Vancouver, and all over the United States where I have attended AA meetings. I am a very lucky person. Without the love of my higher power and of all of these people, I would have shared the fate of my uncle, who died when he was 28 years old. God rest his soul.

Chapter 6

Life Is Good

. . . she had blackouts from the time she started drinking in her

early teens.

In the summer of '81, after my freshman year at Rutgers, my parents called me and asked me to come home from Rhode Island, where I was working a summer job. I insisted that my boss couldn't survive without me (even drunk and hung over). I promised to stop drinking (right!) to take the next semester off and live at home and get some kind of "help." This was their second intervention. Earlier that spring, they made an impromptu visit to my dorm (Clothier sixth floor) after hearing about my 18th birthday in New York City. They heard some story from my brothers that alerted them. This really pissed me off, by the way, because if anyone had problems in my family, it was my alcohol- and drug-using brothers. Anyway, I told them I didn't have a drinking problem and agreed to quit for a month. Thank God I only promised to quit "drinking" and was quite successful, as there were a multitude of alternatives to get me through. I graded myself and passed. Three weeks into my one-month commitment was spring break. I was on a plane to San Francisco to visit an old high school boyfriend, drank on the way there, and arrived in a blackout. But that didn't count, did it? After all, it was spring break.

Going to Rutgers meant drinking freely. At home, no one drank but my two older brothers. I was the good girl. I didn't make much noise, and I tried to be helpful.

So, although I started drinking when I was 13, my parents were unaware of it, except on a few occasions when my planning was poor and I drank too much. In the beginning, alcohol found me. It really was an accident. My first drink was a Piña Colada. I fell in love with the boy next door who gave it to me, and two addictions started simultaneously. The relationship with the boyfriend lasted for four years, and my drinking continued for seven, into the fall of my sophomore year at Rutgers. I never did take a legal drink in the state of New Jersey. Right now I have 22 years of sobriety and counting. I count because I have been sober more than half of my life. Sober three times longer than I drank, and 22 years away from the reality of what happens to me when I drink.

Or maybe it was an adolescent phase?

Drinking at 13 is tricky. I don't wish this on any child. I had to drink early on Saturday mornings so I was sober enough to go home for dinner. Parents' being away was always a party. Summer camp also became an opportunity. At 13, I had my first blackout in Maine. Lots of cold beer going down quickly never felt so good. The next thing I remember is waking up in my bunk. My first thought always fascinates me when I think back on it. I was angry, angry about someone putting me to bed because I didn't remember doing it myself. What a feeling to walk through the pine trees the next morning, recalling nothing. I kept my ears open but didn't hear anything horrible, so I assumed that nothing bad happened. Right about this time, I'm thinking that alcohol may just be a bit dangerous for me.

I had many blackouts over the years. Another one was at a Caribbean sailing camp. I was a little older, and this time my boat mates made sure I knew how obnoxious I was when I was drunk. Our skipper had a bottle of, what the hell was it, some top-shelf drink, like Crown Royal, I think. The "Captain's Drink." The rule was that you were allowed to drink from this incredibly beautiful and potent bottle whenever you were steering the boat. So we pulled into some small cove that was famous for its homemade rum drinks with fresh nutmeg grated on top. I bet they are still serving them today. In a blackout, before we left the shore, I proceeded to hang off the sides of the boat and was singing and shouting, irritating everyone. They probably wished I would have fallen in. There's an interesting thought. It was also on this trip that I had that "oh so very special" first opportunity to wake up next to someone I had no intention of sleeping with. Maybe nothing happened. About this time, I'm wondering how much I care about losing bits and pieces of my life.

I blacked out once again on Thanksgiving Eve and this time performed for my whole family. I crawled into my house, past my teetotaling grandparents, who were in town for the holiday, crawled up the stairs, and proceeded to throw up all over the bathroom. My mother put me to bed in a little bunk under my usual bed, and when I woke up I again, I got angry. My sister was angrier, and then she explained what had happened the night before. This was going to be a big punishment from Dad. Tearfully lying and saying it was the first time I ever drank, I guess I overdid it, and I had broken up with my boyfriend did the trick. No consequences. Right about now, I am marveling at the benefits of telling a good lie. (I love you, Dad.)

In the spring of my senior year of high school, I was driving. Drinking and driving. Blacking out and driving. I drove my parents' station wagon. I didn't wreck it, which was a plus. We didn't die in it, either, another plus. One night, I must have been nominated best candidate to drive home, but I have no recollection of it at all. If I don't remember driving the car, who I drove home, or where these people lived, how did I do it? Wasn't this some kind of miracle? Does anybody know how this works? I used to get so freaked out at meetings when I heard truck drivers confess to driving their 18-wheelers up and down the New Jersey Turnpike every day in complete blackouts. At least I wasn't that bad, was I?

Then there are always the fun blackouts, like waking up in the middle of the night, peeing in my college roommate's closet, and her yelling, "What the hell are you doing?" Too bad we were in her mother's house over the Jewish Holiday. Right about this time, I'm thinking, this might be a problem.

So in my short seven years of drinking, there were blackouts. More and more bits and pieces of my life I couldn't account for. Any feelings I had regarding the blackouts had to be dismissed because they were simply the price I had to pay to continue going into oblivion. Ahhhhhhhhh, to drink into oblivion. I loved that.

In the 10th grade, my first boyfriend was involved in a sexual crime that became public. It involved three other boys and a girl, who also happened to be a neighbor of ours. Damn. I was madly in love and dependent on him, and this really messed me up. I continued to see him secretly for a while. How would I ever cope with this? Oh yeah, I remember now. I went to my best friend and finally converted to drinking and drugging. "Let's go! It's time to get high." Up until this point, I had avoided drugs because I had made a distinction in my mind between alcohol and drugs. Drugs didn't fit into the good girl's image.

I made this same distinction during my first nine months in AA, too. "All you have to do is stop drinking; you can do anything except that." I'm good as long as I have my pot, acid, and cocaine. Besides, how else was I supposed to unwind from final exams? Don't get me wrong. I wasn't a drug addict. I used these drugs socially and responsibly. Getting accidentally pregnant and needing to get high before going to work in the summer of '82 changed my mind a bit. So now, I'm pretty close to bottom.

I accidentally celebrated my first year anniversary in AA with only three months being drug free. It was at this big speaker meeting on Saturday night, I think, at Six Mile Run. I kind of hated that meeting. It must have had 100 people in it, smoking away. Dotty was always trying to get me to mix with the young people there. "Don't you want to go bowling?" Can't we just go the meeting and get this over with? There was this little old, skinny man named George who used to greet us at the door, smiling and hugging us as we went in—really squeezing. Do we really have to do this? Then Dotty used to ask me to pick up the repulsive ashtrays. I was so out of it, I just did what she said. You can see why I hated this place. I figured out I wasn't

58

supposed to get high and celebrate sober anniversaries in AA (this is brain surgery), and I went back to Six Mile Run and coughed up the truth on my true anniversary. By this time, you can probably guess, I had taken up bowling.

Back to the summer of '81, when I was living in a Rhode Island with my cousin; It was heaven on earth. This was going to be my new life. No history haunting me; a chance to recreate myself. The starting gun went off, and the next thing I know, I wake up next to a coworker—the wrong coworker. Don't you hate that? I publicly swore off drinking to try and redeem a scrap of self-respect in my brand-new life. So I wouldn't drink for a week. Great, I can do this. Time to reward myself with a nice bottle of wine, at home, alone. No way to humiliate myself doing that, right? Until I forgot to pick up my cousin from work, seven miles away from home. She banged on the wall six inches from my head, trying to wake me. Why I locked the door was another mystery. We had no keys.

I woke up one day and said to my cousin that I just couldn't take "it" any more. She suggested that we call our uncle, who was in AA. No thanks. THAT wasn't my problem. Our uncle was nuts. I remember the day he announced himself to us. We were at a big family gathering in the country. He was so friendly for a stranger, it was offensive. No one in his right mind could be that happy. (I love you, Uncle Dick.)

I continued to control my drinking that last summer. That is, if we can consider the word *control* accurate. I stopped at a bar to have just one drink on my way home after a long, hard day of work and woke up on a boat in the harbor.

I was asked to leave by the lady I was living with. Evicted at 18. I bet she was in Al-Anon. I loved her. She let us rent her hunting lodge on the back of her property and gave us her pickup to drive. (Remember drinking and driving, blacking out and driving?) She liked me but said that I needed to go. We were in a tiny town. Of course, she heard stories about me from the locals, but she said I wasn't taking care of myself, and she wasn't in a position to do it for me. I couldn't argue with that.

So Mom called me and asked me to leave the island and meet them on vacation. We negotiated. I agreed to take a semester off from Rutgers and to get help. I promised not to drink the rest of the summer. Right.

Twenty years of therapy started that fall. My first therapist and I started to talk about my life, my position in my family, the middle child, how I didn't get what I needed from my parents, and how I just might be really angry at my mom without knowing it, maybe even hated her. (I love you, Mom.) She didn't care that I drank. She was going to help me to uncover all the issues that led me to drinking, to get to the bottom of my troubled life. I always felt worse after seeing her, like an alien walking around on earth, like WTF is going on around here? I learned one thing from her, that a person needs therapy if he ever feels helpless and hopeless at the same time. Thanks a bunch.

The next thing I know, I'm looking in the yellow pages under Alcoholism Counselor. Yes, my new life began with Bell Atlantic. That's Verizon for all of you new kids. I don't know whatever possessed me. My fingers did the walking, and we found Richard. Richard was mild mannered. He was soft spoken, and he had a legal-size yellow tablet. He knew we would need it to list all of the drugs I had ever used. He told me WTF was going on in my other therapy. She would try and straighten my past out to fix my drinking, and he would fix my drinking, which would straighten everything out. Alcoholism was a D-I-S-E-A-S-E, he said.

We met weekly that fall. I made these little drinking/drugging deals with him. I thought two drinks was a reasonable amount, and maybe getting high once every three weeks or so wouldn't be such a big deal. His technique was brilliant—pure torture. St. Patrick's Day was oh-so-fun that spring. Not! So I did this controlling thing. I was honest with Richard. Bye-bye to Oblivion, my best friend.

What was I going to do to control myself at Rutgers?

Hmmmmm. Richard suggested AA meetings during our therapy, but remember the cult Uncle Dick was sucked into? I don't think so. I also saw a meeting book in his office. It was worse than I thought: a religious cult. The last little deal I made with him was to see if Rutgers had a group for students who wanted to control their drinking. If not, I promised to try AA as a last resort. I knew this would also mean the end to my life. It wasn't a great life, but I would be sorry to see it go.

Sure enough, there was no group. Whoever I spoke to at Rutgers said that they were thinking of starting a group but didn't have one in place yet. Great. I guess they took my number, because at some point I began sitting around a little table with someone who was trying to get a master's degree in social work or alcoholism counseling or something and a compulsive-talking, tattooed, reformed drug addict and alcoholic. Forgive me if someone else was in the room that first day. The tattoos were so shocking to me, and I'm sure hardly anyone got a chance to speak. I do remember that, over time, more and more students entered the room, but we were still all able to fit around that little table in a back room up on the third floor of one of the Rutgers University Health Services buildings.

In the meantime, I kept my word with Richard and was trying AA in New Brunswick. (Oh yeah, I love you, Richard.) My first AA meeting was almost my last. The same woman who told me that Rutgers didn't have a group for students recommended a meeting in some kind of AA club downtown. I went looking for this meeting by myself and found some old men, seemingly unemployed, smoking cigarettes and playing cards. No, thank you. Time to Run Away.

The secretary was redeemed when shortly thereafter I went to a lunch meeting on the Busch campus. The meeting ran over, and I was late for my class, so I asked the first woman I saw rushing out of the room if she could give me a lift across the river. Dotty. There were a lot of Dotties in those days, and I got one of them. She asked me how long I had been coming to AA, and when I told her it was my first meeting, she said there was another great meeting that night and would I like to go with her? A great meeting? I don't think so. I was so out of it I said, sure, so my first day in AA, I went to two meetings. Now Dotty used to take me to all my meetings, and I was never suspicious of how far away these meetings were. They needn't have been. (My mom was suspicious of Dotty, though. Who was this stranger? And be careful!) I know it was her trap to get me to talk. We spent all this time talking in the car, and she debriefed me on all the topics and questions I had for that day, the God thing in particular. (Just keep an open mind). I still carry so many thoughts of Dotty around with me. I loved it when I told her the whole program really seemed like brainwashing, and she roared with laughter, saying, "Let's face it, Honey; your brain could use a little scrubbing!" She was also quitting smoking when I met her. Another Dotty slogan I used over the years is, "If I can quit, anybody can quit." (I love you, Dotty.)

The director of the university recovery program sent me to Sheila, a psychiatrist, to help me deal with "problems other than alcohol": an incestuous sexual molestation that transpired over several years of my childhood. I thought I was supposed to be getting better, and now I was hauling myself down to Red Bank for therapy. So, Sheila, just how does a person deal with this? She prescribed one Al-Anon meeting a week to assist with our therapy. I was in my third year of sobriety, and now I'm sentenced to Al-Anon. Great. Sheila helped me move on. She brought me into the present. This therapy would need way more than one sentence to describe, but I'll leave it at that. I was also engaged to someone in AA at this time. He was a great distraction, and I was in danger of not graduating after five years of attending Rutgers. Sheila helped me there, too. The ring was off before final exams. Many, many weights were lifted during this time. Thank you. (I love you, Sheila.)

Rutgers, meanwhile, had started their student recovery group. Our little table meeting was transforming into massive group therapy. There were so many of us and so little of the one director. How she put up with all of our crap, I will never

62

know. Somehow, she managed to glue us together week after week, year after year. I believe she helped to build that bedrock we all needed to get where we are today. It is astounding how many of us from that original group have over 20 years of sobriety now. She suggested that we start a meeting on College Avenue, so we did. Same phenomenon. Little table upstairs meeting blows through auditorium. Am I the only one who needed the director of the program after graduation? She had a little private practice, you know. I found it, and there was always an appointment available when I needed one. How did she ever have the time? Rutgers, you should have paid her more so she didn't have to work after work! (I love you, Lisa.)

Life at school felt like an outpatient rehab between '83 and '85. Individual therapy weekly, group therapy weekly, on-campus AA meeting weekly, and whatever other meetings we frequented. We poured so much love and attention into each other. Our reunions are fantastically warm. Velvet. (I love you guys.)

Fast forward. I finally graduated, married a man in AA, had my first daughter, went into my first business with my husband, lost my second child midterm, had my second daughter, sold my first business, separated from my husband the first time, got back together, went into my second business,[1] separated a second time, and just recently sold the second business.

I'm currently living with my two girls on the eve of a divorce after three years of being separated. (Must have been those severe emotional twists that weren't eliminated or those deep-lying emotional handicaps, rising up under pressure to handicap us.[2]) I'm a bit exhausted just thinking about it all and am back in therapy, trying to help myself complete the tasks at hand. Single motherhood. Many do it. I don't wish it on anyone. Life is too full sometimes, and balancing is always tricky. Coping with it all is the constant challenge. Coping without chemicals.

I've never left AA. I'm still scrubbing after 22 years, attending weekly step meetings, secretary of one, sponsoring two women, and being sponsored. I attend Al-Anon. A few weeks ago, I was with a friend in the program who is in early recovery and was feeling particularly hopeless. So I pointed out the promises in the "Big Book" and gave her some of mine. It works for me.

---

[1] Definition of insanity.

[2] I don't believe that there was anything wrong in our marriage that couldn't have been fixed by working the steps. Antidotes to just about all relationship issues are in there. It does, however, require both partners' cooperation and concerted effort. (I love you. Al-Anon.)

Chapter 7

A Cut Next To the Rest

. . . she drank to get drunk, even though no one in her family was an alcoholic, and found a release from overwhelming feelings through cutting herself.

I am the only one in my family who is an alcoholic. My parents and siblings are social drinkers, if that. I, however, never drank socially. When I drank, my goal was to get to a state of drunkenness where my intense emotions for the world, externally and internally, would be numbed so I would not have to be so afflicted with the world's worries.

As I look back, even as a child I was very aware of the world and all of its cares, in addition to my immediate social circles and all of their cares. I have always considered myself to be a deeply feeling person with a "super sense" of issues and events.

In addition to this "super sense," my family life was one of emotional and mental turmoil. My father was very domineering; it was his way or no way, and he was also often moody (Jekyll and Hyde). Now, as an adult, I would say he is mentally ill, perhaps bipolar. As a result of this, I never knew what type of mood he would be in and, therefore, how to behave. As an example, I came home excited from my high school soccer game, where I was the goalie and captain of the team. We had won the game, and my father asked who on my team scored the goals. I could not recall, and as a result, my father hit me, which ended up with my having a bit of a black eye. Physical abuse was not very prevalent in our household, but mental and emotional manipulation was. My teen years were very lonely and confusing years for me.

I started drinking as a junior in high school. However, about a year prior to that, I began to engage in behavior that today is called *self-harm behavior* or *cutting*. I found it to be a wonderful release. I continued this behavior throughout my drinking years. When I did start to drink, it was with the sole intent to get drunk. Because I was only 16 or 17 years old and living at home, my opportunities for drinking were few, but when they arose, I took full advantage of them.

For two summers during my drinking years, I worked at a private pool and tennis club as the lead cook in the snack bar. The food area closed about an hour and a half before the club did, which gave my coworkers and me a perfect setting to drink—in the picnic area of the club.

Once I started college (Rutgers College of Engineering), my drinking significantly increased. I was away from home, responsible only for myself, and there was always someone of age who was willing to purchase alcohol for me. Looking back, I believe I drank six days of every week during that first semester in college. I definitely drank more than most of the students in my dorm, and also handled it much better (high tolerance).

During that first semester, I also went to join the women's soccer team, which was only a club at that time, but the team wasn't very receptive to new people, so I left. However, despite the team's cool welcome, because the position I played was goalie (interesting position; great for someone into self-harm behavior), and the team was often in short supply of that position, the coach would call to see if I could fill in and play. The decision of whether I agreed to play or not depended on whether I had plans to be drinking the night before the game. If so, I would decline the offer, which was often the case. My second year in college, I was a full-time member of the team, and I do recall some great times. Too bad it was not a varsity sport at the time.

As I mentioned earlier, I was attending the College of Engineering, which meant an 18-credit course load, consisting of math and science classes and one elective. Needless to say, drinking and attempting that much course work did not really mix well. For three semesters, I attempted to make it work, but I kept getting further behind. I ended up failing at least one course a semester and was getting Bs, Cs and Ds in the other ones.

During my first three semesters at college, my undiagnosed depression became deeper, and I started feeling suicidal. The drinking and cutting were becoming more frequent; I was drinking more often than not and cutting not only my arm, but also, at times, my face. I even had the idea that I might kill myself through drinking. If it happened, it happened. I didn't care one way or the other. I wasn't so sure I would live to see the age of 21—or, more likely, I didn't care.

Drinking had taken its toll on me physically in just three short years. I was a frequent visitor to the health center at the university, with a host of gastrointestinal symptoms. One of the nurses at the center befriended me, and when she asked if I was drinking and how often, I was honest with her. She had heard of a program that was starting for students with alcohol problems and gave me the information. After that, it was up to me.

At this point, I had seen a couple of therapists and often went to talk with one (or two) of the campus ministers at Christos House (campus ministry), who also befriended me. I clearly knew that there was something wrong with my life. I could out-drink most everyone I knew, was often sick with stomach problems, had an extremely high tolerance for alcohol, was very depressed, continued to cut, did not like many people, disliked life, disliked myself, didn't care too much about things, and found little happiness in anything. So, I figured I would give the student alcohol program a try.

When I went to the place where they were meeting, the group consisted of a counselor and one other student. They asked me if I knew what an alcoholic was, and I stated that I did not. I listened to what they had to say and, strangely, did not feel out of place with them. This was in early November 1982, my third semester at Rutgers.

I continued to go to this group, and by the end of the semester, I think another student or two had joined us. I had stopped my drinking for the most part during this time, but when we were on winter break, I went to a party and tried someone's mixed drink. I liked it and decided to make my own. It did not taste the same, and I did not finish it. That was my last drink— January 8, 1983—no big bang, no last drunk. I guess I was ready to stop, six and a half months into the legal drinking age, which was 19 at that time in New Jersey, and I was done.

When I went back for my fourth semester, I continued to meet once a week with the recovery group on campus. The first student in the group took me to some Alcoholics Anonymous (AA) meetings, and I began to follow that program as well.

During my early recovery, I was still quite depressed; that did not change. The things that did begin to change included feeling physically better, doing okay in my classes, and having a good support group during the semester. Unfortunately, I did not have much support when I went home for the summer, but I did make it through without drinking.

My fifth semester at school started well. I was back in the university recovery program and also going to therapy, but I was still struggling with depression. The semester, in general, was a good one for me. I was feeling a little more positive, enjoying my classes, liking my roommates, and enjoying time spent with my new sober friends. However, I was not doing well in my classes and knew, before the end of the semester, that I would not return the next semester. In my five semesters, grade-point wise, I had my best semester drunk and my worst semester sober.

I quickly found a job at a large global personal products company and shortly thereafter moved in with some sober friends. I worked for a year and decided to reapply to Rutgers as a part-time evening student. I changed my major from Civil Engineering to Psychology, figuring my degree would be more marketable to business and industries. It was nice to be back in school, along with being able to again attend the University recovery program.

The friendships I made in that program were like none I ever had. We had a great group of recovering students and supported each other outside of group and meetings. We had lots of parties, went on camping and canoeing trips, went bowling, played games, and went to concerts and movies. You name it, we planned it and did it. It was the college experience anyone could hope for—and it was all done sober.

Despite all the wonderful experiences, I was still dealing with a level of depression, still cutting myself, but I was no longer feeling suicidal. I really did not know what or how to feel anything other than angry or content (not happy, just content). I even asked my therapist, "What else is there if I am not depressed?" I really didn't know. I tried to be more than content with things and started to feel periodic bouts of joy—which was novel!

In my early sobriety, I came to the realization that I was a lesbian. It was not a big surprise to me or most of my friends. I had some boyfriends here and there. One even thought that, if I went out with him again, I would realize I was not gay. I know that he meant no harm by his comment, that he truly loved me, and only wanted us to be together again.

About 11 years into my recovery, I was hurt very deeply by someone I trusted. This situation led me to a deeper level of my depression. I needed more help than what the program and counseling could offer. Even though I was skeptical that any medication would work, I was in such a bad state, I was willing to try. After some trial and error with different medications, we found one that actually helped–and at a very low dose, to boot. The decision to seek outside help was a very hard one for me to make. Everyone in the program has an opinion regarding pharmaceutical treatment, the predominant one's being that none should be taken. I discussed it with two doctors and a counselor who happened to be in the program, all of whom advised me to take the medicine. After this experience, I realized that AA's focus is on sobriety, and sometimes you need to address medical issues with the appropriate medical professional.

This is not something I chose to discuss as a part of my sobriety in the rooms of AA due to the negative reaction. I chose to mention it here in hopes that someone else who may be experiencing depression will not have to wait as long as I did to get the proper treatment.

I have a lot of "I nevers," and I hope to keep it that way. I never lost a job, family, or friends; never blacked out, got a DWI, or got into legal trouble. I was a high bottom drunk, a very high bottom drunk, relatively speaking. But it was bad enough for me.

Now for the good stuff: what life is like now. I have been sober since 1983 and have accomplished a lot in that time. I earned two college degrees: a Bachelor's and a Master's (with Distinction). I was the symbolic graduate for all of the graduating class from my graduate school. My hard work earned me eligibility into two honor societies. I earned a professional certification and was voted "Member of The Year" three times by my chapter of a professional organization of which I was a board member. I worked at the personal products company I mentioned earlier, for 14 years, earning raises and promotions each year. I have been at my current employer for the past seven years and am doing well here, too. I met the woman I am going to spend my life with; we have been together for over 10 years. We have a fantastic relationship, one built on mutual respect, trust, and honesty, and filled with a lot of humor.

Has everything been so positive in sobriety? Not really; we have had our share of tough situations. Three of our six cats and our first bird have passed away. My partner has gone through four major spinal surgeries and two minor ones and, as a result, is permanently disabled. Given this situation, there are some financial situations that get rough. I also lost a good friend from cancer (too young) and have dealt with other types of losses and life's typical day-to-day situations and have not drunk over them.

Life is life; we handle each situation as it comes and do the best we can. We get through them by not falling into the victim role and by staying proactive and doing what we can. And, again, humor helps a lot.

Life is good today; with all of its ups and downs, it is good. When I was drinking, I thought that if I made it to age 21, that would be good. My goal now is to live a very long and active life. Continuing to stay sober will help me to achieve that goal.

Chapter 8

My Bottom Brought Me to the Top

. . . AA taught him how to love himself.

"What the caterpillar calls the end of the world, the master calls a butterfly."

I thought that recovery was about stopping drinking and using. I feared it like it was my worst enemy. I now know that I was wrong. Recovery can, on a physical level, be about healing the body and, on a spiritual level, about nurturing the soul. But I found out that recovery is about learning to live, instead of just existing in a body. I learned that recovery is about finding a life that works for me, a life based on my own talents, my dreams, and my limits. It's about learning to live my life, not the life others have prepared for me. It's about accepting my sexual orientation. It's also about accepting that I am not perfect and that I am far from it. I have my limits; I have areas in life that I am not good at, such as working with numbers. But I also learned that I don't have to be perfect. I am okay the way I am right here, right now. I don't have to change. I don't have to do anything to be worthy of life. I don't have to do anything to deserve love from others. I am okay the way I am. If others don't like the way I am, then it's their problem, not mine. I can accept myself as a gay recovering alcoholic and addict, and I choose to be with people who accept me for who I am.

Recovery taught me that is okay to make mistakes. I don't have to be right all the time. I have the same rights as everybody on Earth. I don't have to make excuses for my mistakes. I don't have to apologize for my thoughts and feelings. I have the right to be me. I have the right to cry, scream, need things, be loved, love, and be happy and sad. In other words, I don't have to make excuses for being alive and breathing.

For me, recovery was mainly about learning to accept myself for who I am. Accept that I don't have the family I dreamed of. I can't make my family the perfect family by drinking myself to oblivion. I can't make the past go away by indulging myself in cocaine. I realized I needed to change. It started with a little act of kindness to myself. I started saying, "I can't take one more day of insanity." I looked for help, and I was fortunate enough to be a student at Rutgers University. I was able to receive counseling and support from everyone involved in the recovery program. I was introduced to AA. In AA, I started to work the steps with my sponsor. I began to attend meetings and to make commitments. My first sponsor suggested that I start to say "I love you" to my reflection in the mirror. Even though I did not believe my own words, I followed the suggestion.

With time, I realized that nice words did something for me, and, little by little, I learned to love myself. I learned to take care of myself. I learned to like me and to be good to me. It was not something that happened overnight. And it was not easy. It cost me a lot of tears, pain, courage, strength, and faith. There were times I wanted to give up, but I learned in AA that it was at those times that it was most important for me to keep walking and also to reach out to others for help. Even though recovery has cost me a lot of hard work, I strongly believe recovery is worth all the costs.

Today, I choose life in recovery rather than death. Life in recovery for me represents not only having good days, but handling the bad days in a healthy way. It's having faith that the sun will come up again.

Through recovery, I have found a life that works for me. I have learned to speak with my heart instead of with my hatred. I have learned to talk about my needs instead of screaming my needs out under the influence of alcohol and drugs. I have learned to take time to rest and to take care of me. I have learned to trust my gut. Since I began attending AA, I have felt that I have found a new me and made a home out of all the rooms of AA.

Many people feel sorry for me, for wasting away my life in AA, but I have been luckier than many people. At the age of 32, I have learned to know myself. I know my limits, and I know what I am made of. I have fought a very hard battle, but I have also seen what strength I have inside me. I have learned to appreciate all the things my body can do for me. And I don't want to poison it with alcohol and cocaine. I think I have learned many lessons that other people never learn during their lifetime, and, most importantly, I have learned to live in the present. I have learned to cherish each ray of sunshine that comes my way. I have learned not to take life so seriously anymore, that there should be room for playing and laughter.

But I pray to my higher power to never go back there . . . never, never. I have seen what it's like on the other side, and I am not willing to give away the colors of life. I am not willing to throw away the gift of recovery.

I am a grateful Gay Recovering Alcoholic.

Chapter 9

Hey – Wake Up!

. . . her ritual was drink, pass out, wake up, drink. And school

was a blur that she just got through.

"Hey. Wake up. They called on the phone for you. You had a pass; you were supposed to leave ten minutes ago." "Thanks," I mumbled, grabbing my book bag and rubbing my eyes. My head was throbbing. Perhaps a tumor, I speculated. I handed the pass to my teacher and wandered into the hall. "I hope this doesn't take long," I thought. "I don't feel well."

That wasn't much different than any other day, but all the same, I really didn't want to do this. I thought about cutting out early. "Eh. Too much effort. I'll just go down there and bullshit for a while."

So, really, it was laziness that got me into this mess. Well . . . not quite, but about an hour later, I was wishing like hell that I had left school while I still had the chance. I was wishing it even harder an hour after that, as I sat in the back seat of my parents' car on the way to rehab. How had this happened? At the time, it seemed like a complete injustice. I reveled in my victimhood, meditating on the unfairness of my situation and wondering what a nice person like me could have done to deserve such horrible treatment.

There I was, innocently bullshitting my way through one of my many alcohol counseling appointments, when I was completely ambushed. Heads were shaken, calls were made, and I was on my way to some place called Clearbook Lodge. Even worse than that, with the exception of a few gulps I managed during the 10 minutes I'd been given to pack—or, rather, the two minutes out of those 10 when my mom wasn't standing a foot away—I hadn't had a drink since that morning. Not that I needed one, of course. Despite what seemed to be the general consensus of those close to me, I most certainly was not an alcoholic.

Four days later, riding back to rehab from the detox unit they had to rush me to not long after my arrival, I wondered if maybe I didn't need to revise that statement. Four days of shaking, puking, and sweating and countless conversations with doctors and counselors. "No, I don't drink all that often." "No, certainly not every day . . . just once in a while with friends."

None of that was true, of course. Drinking had long since ceased to be social for me. I didn't want to be anywhere near other people when I drank. I didn't want to talk to you, didn't want to have to pretend to have fun, and, most of all, didn't want to share my stuff with you. I drank as much as I could get as quickly as I could get it down—and I did most of it by myself. Not much about it had been fun for the last year or so. So, as I sat there in rehab, and I heard myself lying, I knew how desperate and ridiculous I must have sounded, but the words had become familiar by then.

Still, as I stared out the window, wondering why the scenery didn't look familiar, realizing that I actually couldn't remember much of the ride there, I knew that something was incredibly wrong in my life. If I had been able to take an honest assessment of myself at the time, the picture would not have been pretty: stringy hair, baggy sweatpants complete with stains and burn holes, barely 100 pounds—and the inside was even uglier.

The past year had been a bit of a blur. Drink. Pass out. Wake up. Drink. Figure out how to get more. Repeat. There were other things in there—some school, for instance. But I didn't really care about anything else, and for the last few months, I had stopped bothering to even pretend to care. What had started as a way to feel normal and stop my brain from spinning so fast had turned on me and consumed me. Somewhere between age 11, when I started drinking, and 15, when I wound in that rehab, alcohol beat me, and beat me hard. I felt betrayed, scared. I knew that alcohol was why I was like I was—but still, I was consumed by the desire to drink.

I had plenty of reasons not to drink. But they were in my brain, and only my brain. Every other atom in my body was screaming for a drink. The doctor told me I'd die within five or six years if I didn't stop. So that was bad, right? It should have been, I guess, but at the time, I was just angry that it would take that long. When my brain started to clear up, my counselor told me that if kept drinking I might die—or I might not. He said, "Maybe you'll live. Just like this. For a long time." That terrified me. Every day hurt at that point, and in my 15-year-old brain, death seemed like a valid option.

"How," I began to wonder, "will it ever be different?" It wasn't as if I had never tried to stop drinking before. I would set goals for myself, say, three days with no drinking (other drugs were sometimes and sometimes not included in these abstinence policies).

When I would make these promises, I would genuinely intend to keep them. After a while, though—at first a day or two and eventually just a few hours—I would start to think. The beginning of the end.

"Well, I haven't had a drink for half a day, which proves that I could do it for a whole day if I wanted to," I would reason. "So since I can do it, that means I don't have a problem, and if I don't have a problem, I can drink." It wasn't that I couldn't do it; I just didn't want to right this moment. That's what I told myself, and it made sense every time. Sitting in rehab, though, all of a sudden it didn't seem quite so logical. I couldn't stop drinking. I didn't know about being an alcoholic—that sounded a bit too dramatic and permanent—but I knew that I was out of control. More importantly, I knew that I didn't know what to do about it.

I did well in rehab. I was a master at figuring out what I was supposed to say and then saying it. I wrote insightfully on the steps, shared just enough in meetings, and told everyone else what they should be doing.

When I look back to that time, it's easier for me to see how full of it I was. I lied, manipulated, and tried as hard as I could to hang onto every aspect of the disease that I could without actually drinking. Even as I began to accept that I was an alcoholic, I wasn't sure if I cared. And even in those moments when I did, I had little confidence that I could ever live any differently. All the same though, that stay in rehab was the beginning . . . of something. Did I never take a drink again after that? Nope, not really. I wouldn't really get and stay sober for another two years. But, as they say, the seed had been planted.

When I left rehab, I went to meetings every day for months. I made coffee, got phone numbers (calling them was an entirely different matter), went to diners. I felt horrible. I was depressed, I was angry, and I fought with my family more than I had when I was drinking. Clearly, I figured, AA didn't work. So, I drank. And to make a long story short, I was still an alcoholic. I tried again. Same results. I went back to AA.

Sometimes, I'd hear suggestions and I'd follow them— and maybe I'd even feel a bit better. Most of the time, though, a well- meaning AA member would suggest that I do something, and while I'd thank them for the advice and tell them I'd do it, I rarely would. I thought that those suggestions, like the "12 Steps," were for other people. My superior intellect enabled me to skip over them. It also, incidentally, allowed me not to believe in any type of higher power, as I was sure that that was the ultimate sign of weakness and stupidity.

When I was 17, and had once again become convinced that AA was for suckers and I didn't need it, I went out drinking for what I hoped to God was the last time. The first night was fine, and I woke up the next morning—in my own bed and everything—convinced that what I had thought was alcoholism was actually just youthful experimentation gone awry. I could drink like a normal person. So I did—the next night. Only this time, things didn't work out quite so smoothly. Sometimes, as had happened that first night, I could drink and drink, and not much would happen. Other times, I'd have three or four, and all hell would break loose. I could never predict what would happen when I picked up a drink. That night was one of the latter times. Within a 48-hour period, I'd managed to desert my best friend at some crazy house I had dragged her to, and to have my parents driving across the state and back trying to track me down. When they found me, I threw my car keys at them and tried to talk my way out of trouble. How dare they accuse me of drinking or anything else! The sick thing about my thinking at that point was that I actually was horrified and offended. I lied all the time and I knew I was lying, but if anyone ever questioned my honesty, I was genuinely enraged.

After a few more weeks of this sort of thing, I was given an ultimatum: get sober or get out. Now, my parents are wonderful, loving people, and the last thing they wanted to do was to put me out of the house. But contrary to what I thought when I was drinking, I was hurting everyone around me. They were not going to sit there and watch me kill myself and destroy the family in the process. My initial reaction was one of arrogance and defiance. "Well, then, I'm leaving. I don't need this, and I sure as hell don't need you people." I developed a brilliant plan—or at least what passed for a brilliant plan in my mind. I called a girl I'd been in rehab with who I knew was living about an hour away. She told me that she was staying with her boyfriend, that both of them were dealing drugs, and that I was more than welcome to crash there for a while. "Wow," I thought, "this is all working out so well." I went out to celebrate. I wasn't supposed to be driving at that point, but I told my mom that I needed to go to an AA meeting. I felt a twinge of guilt, but not enough to stop me, and so I drove to a party I'd heard about. I had been really trying to be a social drinker since I'd gone out (social, in my mind, being defined as simply being near other people as I got hammered). I walked in the door and went over to Jim, whose house it was, to say hi. "Yo. What are you doing here?" Not exactly the greeting I'd expected from him. "What?" I asked, "I'm just here, man." He looked uncomfortable. "You can't drink if you're going to be here. I can't get in trouble with my parents again, and I just don't want anything to go wrong."

I felt a mix of shame and anger. "Why would anything go wrong because of me?" I almost asked, but then I remembered the last time I'd been over there, and I decided not to even bother with the question. "Whatever." I started to walk away. "I'm just going to hang out for a minute." So that's what I did. I had two beers on the sly (what normal person has to sneak drinks at a party where everyone is getting trashed?), played designated driver for someone who had left their wallet at home, and then left the party. I had never liked any of those people, I reminded myself.

There wasn't really anyone I did like at that moment. People in AA were full of it. Hadn't I just gone to a party and had two drinks? "Can't drink normally my ass," I mumbled to myself. I knew what I'd do. I still had a fifth of vodka in my drawer at home, just in case, and I decided to go home and comfort myself with that. After all, it had been a bad night. Even as I made that decision, I felt the tension start to leave my body. The anger and loneliness and fear faded and were replaced with a sense of relief and anticipation. I drove home, locked myself in my room, got drunk, and convinced myself that this was exactly how I had really wanted to spend my night all along.

A week later, I was back in rehab once again. I wish that I had a good story for how this happened, a nice spiritual awakening or something of that nature, but really all that happened was that I realized how weak and sick I was for a split second. I knew with more certainty than I'd felt about anything in a long time that if I left to go stay with this friend of mine and continue drinking, I would ultimately end up miserable, sick, and alone, just like I always had until that point. Nothing would change, I wouldn't prove anything to anyone, and if I was lucky enough, I'd eventually have to come crawling home to beg for help. In that moment, before my mind could catch up, I called the rehab I'd been in two years earlier and begged them to take me back.

They didn't have a bed, but they knew me well and told me to come, anyway, that they would work something out. If I had had to wait, I'm sure I would have talked myself out of it. It's not as if I hadn't come to similar realizations about the destructiveness of my drinking before and reneged on them the next morning. So they put me on a cot and, once again, Clearbrook Lodge was my home. It was harder this time, though—a lot harder. When I walked back into rehab, I wasn't in the worst shape of my life. I wasn't failing out of school (although I did manage to set the record that year for number of days late), I wasn't physically beaten up too badly, and while my parents were ready to wash their hands of me, I wasn't in any serious trouble. From the outside, I was in better shape in many respects than I had been the first time I walked through those doors two years earlier. But something was different. I may not have appeared it, but I was broken. Emotionally, spiritually, whatever you want to call it, I felt hopeless in a way that I had never felt before. For perhaps the first time in my life, I truly was out of ideas, out of plans, and I didn't have any answers. I had been powerless over alcohol since I touched it. My life had been unmanageable for long before that, but until that point, I had never been able to admit that to myself. Just as the Big Book describes, I was unable to imagine my life with alcohol or without it.

I didn't recognize it then, but it was at that point that I surrendered. I gave up the fight—not because I thought I could get better or because I didn't want to get worse, but because I was so completely lost and didn't have the energy left to struggle. If I hadn't been in that rehab, I'm not sure what would have happened. Not only did I not want to drink or be sober, but I didn't particularly want to live. I thought about suicide a lot that first few weeks, but even that seemed like it would take too much energy. Ideally, I thought, I would die without having to do it myself. It would be easier on everyone if I were hit by a bus or something. It sounds funny to me now, but at the time, I really walked around hoping for a freak accident—a piano falling on my head or something of that nature. That was my idea of a plan.

I honestly don't know exactly when things started to change. The two weeks I was supposed to spend at Clearbrook were quickly extended to two months. They didn't let me get away with much of anything this time, and because I was so exhausted from how I had been living, I didn't really try too hard to do so. For the first time in what felt like forever, I paid more attention to how I was doing than to how I appeared to be doing. When I felt crazy, I said that I felt crazy, rather than trying to act like everything was fine. It didn't make for a pleasant two months. I would go from laughing to being enraged to being completely depressed, all in the space of half an hour and often without really being sure why. My emotions were all over the place. It had been so long since I had expressed anything I felt normally that I didn't really know how to do it, and so everything came out twisted and sideways, and it left me feeling like I was going out of my mind.

That said, I did make a lot of progress during those two months. I started working the steps, as opposed to just regurgitating what I had read in the literature and heard in meetings. I faced a lot of things that were difficult to face, and I learned to trust people in a way that I had never really been able to do. Again, it didn't necessarily feel good, but I was starting to get better—or at least to believe that maybe I could.

All through this process, I had assumed that, once I completed the program at Clearbrook, I would be sent home. My counselor and my parents, however, had other plans. It was decided that I wasn't ready to return home. After all, how many times had it seemed like I had changed until I was let loose again? I didn't even trust myself, so it wasn't particularly shocking that no one else trusted me. They told me that they had found a halfway house for me and that I needed to go live there for a few months before I could come home. I put up a halfhearted fight, but it was more for show than anything else. If

I had learned nothing else in rehab, I had discovered that I was incredibly sick and that I was incapable of making myself better on my own. I went to the halfway house.

Within days of my arrival, I regretted not putting up more of a fight. The halfway house had a lot more rules than I had expected, and I had always secretly believed that not all rules should apply to me. I also felt that I had a solid grasp of which ones should and which ones should not: Everyone else had to go to school while they were there, but I clearly should not be required to do so; everyone else could smoke only ten cigarettes a day, but I really needed more, and so it should be overlooked when I snuck a few extra. The rules that suited me, those that I understood the point of—going to meetings every day, using the phone only during designated times—I would follow. But if I thought that a rule was stupid, I immediately gave myself license to ignore it.

It sounds silly, but this was actually a real roadblock for me. In order to get sober, I had to do a lot of really difficult things based almost entirely on the faith that the people telling me to do it knew what they were talking about. Until I was able to trust people enough to believe that they knew better than I did what was good for me at that moment, I didn't really change much. I was still trying to control everything. In theory, I had accepted that I didn't know how to manage my own life, but when it came down to the day-to-day application of that concept, I frequently fell far short. At the halfway house, I had to really learn to let go of that and do what they told me, whether or not I thought that it would help me stay sober.

It turns out that they did know what they were talking about. Altogether, I spent about eight months in that halfway house, and I think I needed every day of it. Rehab had given me two months of sobriety and a decent foundation, but I don't know that I would have been able to return home and maintain it. Sure, I would have had AA meetings to go to, but I had gone to nine or ten a week at some points and still gone out and drunk. Until I got honest with myself and became willing to change, I wasn't going to get sober. At the halfway house, where I was constantly focused on recovery and completely removed from anything I could use to distract myself, I was finally able to do this.

In addition, once I stopped doing everything in my power to destroy my life and started showing the tiniest bit of effort and willingness, doors began to open that I wouldn't have dreamed could exist for me. In spite of my best efforts to avoid going, I ended up graduating from high school while I was in the halfway house, and I decided that I did want to go to college.

It was at this point that I learned about the existence of the recovery house at Rutgers. One of my counselors had attended a summer seminar at the university and suggested that I check out the program. Humoring him (I knew I didn't have the grades to get into Rutgers), I called and set up an appointment. At the time, I remember being more excited about the fact that I got an extended home pass from my halfway house so that I could attend the appointment than I was about the possibility of actually living there.

Somewhere during the process of trying to convince the director of the house and the dean at Rutgers College of my sincere desire to live in the sober dorm and attend school, I actually developed those feelings. It's not that I was disinterested before, but just that I never really believed that it would happen. When I started to see that it was a real possibility, I began for the first time to really feel that being sober wasn't a liability, but a gift.

For whatever reason—and despite what I thought at the time, I'm sure it wasn't my superior power of persuasion—I was accepted to Rutgers as a part-time student and allowed to move into the sober apartments. There, I met people my age who had multiple years of sobriety and seemed pretty happy about their lives. They were welcoming and genuine and fun—which was important, because when I got sober I really didn't think that I would ever have fun again. During the three years I spent in recovery housing, I made better friends than I ever could have dreamed possible and had more fun than I had had in years.

What was even more amazing to me was that not only did I have a great time, but I found out that I could be responsible as well—and that it felt good to do so. I went from just getting by (and sometimes not getting by) in high school to graduating Rutgers with highest honors. Even more importantly, I found things that I loved to do and began to set goals and take steps toward reaching them. When I was drinking, I had always dreamed about what I wanted to do with my life, but those dreams were either unrealistic (often to the point of delusion) or unlikely to happen because I wasn't willing to put any actual effort into them. For instance, I used to always talk about traveling when I was drinking, but I never had any money or any energy to even get out of New Jersey. Since I have gotten sober, I have had the opportunity to travel across the United States and to several other countries. I have had experiences that I never would have had if I were drinking, and if it has been this good so far, I can only imagine what will happen if I continue to stay sober and work a program.

My problem is never, as I had expected it to be in early sobriety, that I have nothing to do, but instead that I have too many things that I want to experience in what now feels like never enough time. My life is full. Not only has sobriety given me the opportunity to succeed and build a decent life for myself materially, but it has also given me the ability to have quality relationships with other human beings. Today, I am no longer a burden to my family. I have great friends and a truly wonderful boyfriend whom I would trust with my life—and who feel the same way about me.

If I had to describe what my life would be like today when I had first gotten sober, or even when I had first come to Rutgers, I would have shortchanged myself. It's not that everything is perfect or that I don't still have a lot of work to do on myself (incidentally, I also learned in sobriety that being perfect is not a realistic goal). Going through the steps of the AA program and living a sober life for the past six years has changed me enormously for the better, but I make mistakes all the time. The difference today is that I care and that I am trying to live my life in a way that isn't harmful—to myself or anyone else.

I've also seen what is waiting for me if I do lose sight of what is important. Out of about eight or ten people I was really close to when I first got sober, two are dead, one is in jail, and with the exception of me, the rest are living in extremely difficult situations due to their addictions. As far as I have come from how I was when I was drinking, I know in my heart that I could go right back to the insanity in an instant. I am still an alcoholic, and if I don't keep going to AA and growing spiritually, I will eventually drink again. I have seen it happen, and I have no reason to think that I would be an exception.

For now, I plan on just doing what I have been doing. As I'm writing this, a lot is about to change in my life—all of it good, but a lot of it frightening nonetheless. I only hope that I will be able to take the wonderful and oftentimes very difficult lessons I have learned over the course of the past six years and continue to stay sober and enjoy the wonderful life I have been given.

Chapter 10

Smart in School

. . . she was a good student, a popular classmate, and a pothead

until she found the miracle of recovery.

As I sit down to write this, I am two days away from celebrating 17 years clean and sober. At times, I am struck by what a miracle it is to be sober today. I can feel how real and ingrained my "old life" was. Other times, I am amazed to think about the person I was because my life today is so far removed from a life that has alcohol and other drugs at its core. Recovery is truly one of life's miracles.

I grew up in a rural area of southern New Jersey. My parents remained married until my father's death, which occurred when I was 14. My mother refers to me as her "change of life" baby. I have three older siblings who are between 7 and 12 years older than me.

My mother was primarily a housewife, who at times took temporary office jobs. My father worked rotating shifts at a power plant. I don't remember my parents ever fighting. We had a cabinet that was always stocked with liquor, and there was always beer in the fridge. My father drank regularly. As a kid, I thought this was normal. My father always met his family responsibilities and was never violent. To my knowledge, he did not spend time in bars. As I began to learn about alcoholism, I could see the ways that my father's use of alcohol affected his life. When there were stressful times in the family, his drinking increased. I remember times that his behavior was impaired by his drinking. My mother tells me today that his drinking may well have led them to an eventual divorce.

I first remember drinking beer when I was a little girl. I

would be sent to the refrigerator to get my father his beer. As I brought it to him, I would open the bottle and drink from it. People thought this was cute. When I got older, I followed the path of my siblings by sneaking beer and liquor from the cabinet. I also learned about pot from my siblings.

My boundaries were not very strong as a child. I thought nothing of going through my sister's things and reading her diary. As a result of my snooping, I learned that she was smoking pot. I had seen information at school about pot and the horrible things it did to people. I was worried that my sister was a drug addict because she smoked pot. I would crush her joints the same way I crushed my parent's cigarettes. I'm not sure when, but at some point I started stealing her joints instead.

I was first caught with pot when I was about 11. I had taken pot and a pipe from my sister's stash. My mother asked me what I had in my pockets. I told her it was bubble gum. When she had me empty my pockets, she saw what I really had. She concluded that this meant I didn't have enough to do with my time. She assigned me a task of sewing a pantsuit. I didn't get past cutting out the pattern. I give her an "A" for effort.

My mother was also the youngest child in her family. She says this is why she would have my brothers and sister take me with them on outings rather than leave me behind. My friends and I had already been experimenting with alcohol, pot, and cigarettes. Now I began getting high with my siblings and their friends.

By the time I was 14, I had started smoking cigarettes daily and drinking most weekends. High school opened up a new world of social connections for me. I got stoned every day during the summer after my freshman year and was quite proud of this. This was also the summer that my father died.

My father had come home from work and had a couple of boilermakers (beer mixed with vodka). Work called and needed him to come back in. He was less than five miles from the house when he hit a tree. The road curved, and he didn't make the curve. They say he died instantly. We don't know what happened. Did he fall asleep? Have a heart attack? No one knows. I blamed myself for years. I feared that I had been disappointing him, that this caused him to drink more and led to his accident. He had high expectations for me, and I was beginning to let him down. I was no longer his "little girl"; I was becoming rebellious and not coming home when I was supposed to. My mother was constantly questioning me about my red eyes. My father put a bottle of Murine on my dresser when he came home from work that night. I saw him come in, but I was in bed and didn't say anything. That was the last time I saw my father.

After sobriety, I was able to understand that he made his own choices. If he was upset with me, it's not my fault or responsibility how he dealt with that. I still miss him, yet I wonder if our relationship would have drastically declined as my behavior got worse in the years to follow.

My mother and I were not close growing up. I was a Daddy's girl. After Dad died, Mom and I were thrown together. She was left to grieve the sudden loss of her husband of 30 years, as well as deal with an adolescent with a blooming addiction.

My high school years were somewhat of a contradiction in terms. I was a pothead, and I was an academic student. I was doing angel dust (or THC as we called it), and I was student conductor of the concert band. I was taking LSD, and I was captain of the color guard. I didn't quite fit in anywhere. I didn't feel that I fit in with the straight kids because my family was different (potheads, hippies, lesbians), and I was different. Yet I didn't fit in with the other kids because my family also had a proper streak (my extracurricular activities, a homemaker mother in the DAR, an emphasis on academics). I managed to find kids from both worlds whom I could relate to, but I never had a solid place where I belonged.

During my high school years, I initially had some degree

of restraint. I can remember saying, "I'll smoke pot, but I'll never do speed." Then a friend would suggest I try speed. "Okay, I'll do speed, but I'll never do LSD." Then a friend would suggest I try LSD. Eventually, I realized that I really couldn't absolutely say there was anything I'd never do. If I had a friend who had done it and they said it was okay, then I was willing to do it. I didn't really care what it was or what it would do to me. I had long since decided that all those warnings about drugs weren't real because none of the things they'd told me about pot years ago seemed to be true. The one thing that did scare us all was what we called "banging"—shooting drugs. I had made pacts with friends that if we heard the other had started "banging," we'd "kick their ass."

I was drum majorette during my junior year. This caused a dilemma my senior year. Since I'd already been drum majorette, I decided to do something different. I became a band manager (carrying equipment, etc., for the band). This lasted until I was caught smoking pot in the bathroom at one of the football games and was kicked out. I had also been caught with pot on a weekend away for a state championship marching competition. I was confined to my room for the remainder of the weekend.

My parents felt very strongly about college. So far, none of my siblings had graduated. With my father dead, I couldn't argue the issue with him. I knew this was important to him and felt I had to do it. In May of my senior year, I applied to three colleges at Rutgers University New Brunswick, New Jersey. I wasn't particularly motivated for college, but no other plans had presented themselves. I did fairly well on my SATs the first time I took them. I retook them with hopes of raising my score, but actually did worse the second time (perhaps the LSD I did the night before had something to do with this?). I managed to graduate from high school in 1981. My oldest brother gave me an ounce of pot for graduation. By my senior year in high school, I had begun to tire of pot, and on some level I was disappointed with my brother's gift ("This is what your send me to my future with?"). I was accepted to two of the three schools I applied to.

Rutgers favored my going to Douglass, so that's what I did.

The summer after my senior year, a friend of mine introduced me to shooting speed (methamphetamine). I had never felt as right with the world as I did when I shot speed. I had snorted it before but wasn't so impressed. I was in love with this feeling, and at the same time, I felt I had crossed a big line. High on speed, I would sit in my room and journal for hours on end, often well in to the morning. The contradictions of my life had gone to a new level. Now I was college co-ed and junkie.

I went to Douglass as planned. I was not the best student. My grades were erratic. I'd average a 3.7 one semester and a 1.3 the following semester. I was put on academic probation and assigned a class on study skills. My study skills could use some work, but that wasn't the real problem. It was more likely the gallon bottles of wine we were drinking, the other drugs that came and went, and my general attitude. My RA became my connection for drugs at college. When I was able to get speed, I would go down to the study rooms in the basement and shoot up. I hated my little secret, but I loved the way it made me feel.

Summers home were absolutely crazy. After the independence of college, I had even less restraint at home. After two summers of fighting with my mother, I decided it was time to move to New Brunswick. I became roommates with a friend of my RA's. My drinking and drug use were getting worse. I was coming home drunk, doing drugs in the house, and bringing people to the house who may have made my roommate nervous. She drank and did drugs, but she managed much more decorum than I did.

It was during this time that I hit my first bottom. While home on Christmas break, I met a woman who had just come upon a settlement of money. This woman liked to do speed as much as I did and now had two or three thousand dollars of essentially found money. She was looking for someone to party with, and I was up to the task. We went on a seven- or eight-week speed binge that ended when I fell asleep behind the wheel of her car. This accident resulted in her being in a coma for three days and traction for several weeks. She nearly died. My injuries were minor.

Up to this point, I could convince myself that I had control of my drinking and drug use. I always showed up for work, I always paid my bills, and I wasn't stealing or turning tricks. I knew my life wasn't quite right, but I didn't think it was so bad, either. This woman and her settlement allowed me to see just how far I'd go if money weren't an issue. I totally blew off the first several weeks of the semester. I was staying in my hometown partying while my mother thought that I was at school. I could have killed us in this accident. This was my first real scare. This was February of 1984.

In May of 1985, the semester my Douglass friends were graduating, I was academically dismissed from school. There had been too many bad semesters, and my good semesters could no longer redeem me. I got a job that summer as the Aquatics Director for a summer camp. I became the director of this agency's after-school childcare program the following fall.

I moved from my shared apartment to a communal house with nine other women. I had met women who lived in this house at the bar I frequented. Most of these women led a lifestyle more like mine. My first night at the house, a new roommate of mine stopped by to introduce herself. Before the night was over, we were shooting drugs together. I'd found a place where I didn't have to hide the way I was living. Not only were the alcohol and other drugs accepted, it was also a house of creative, intelligent, and eccentric women. I felt I'd found my home. As Dickens would say, "It was the best of times; it was the worst of times." Eventually we were evicted from this house because it didn't meet housing codes. Some of the women decided to squat there for a while. One night, I went back to the house with the woman who'd welcomed me my first night there. We went to my old room to shoot cocaine (it had become more accessible than speed at this point). She overdosed. I didn't know what to do. I was high, and had no phone to call for help. I tried to give her mouth to mouth and CPR. I could tell it was not effective. I went for help. The ambulance came. I stashed the remaining drugs and went to the hospital. When it was time to leave the hospital, I went back to the house and finished the drugs. She died three days later. This was my second bottom. This was December 1985.

At this point, I really started to feel conflicted about my drug use, in addition to dealing with a lot of grief and pain around my friend's death. I sought counseling at an agency covered by my health insurance. After meeting with me, they told me that I needed to attend groups there three times a week, for three hours a night, at $35 a visit. I thought this was absolutely absurd. I didn't do it.

I looked into what I needed to do for readmission to school. I needed to attend summer school successfully for two summers before I could apply for readmission. I did this. Meanwhile, I kept my job directing swimming and after-school childcare. I enjoyed this job, which surprised me. I had considered childcare to be too traditional a line of work for me, but I really enjoyed it. I was still drinking and doing drugs. I would never miss work, but sometimes I would come to work without having slept at all the night before. When I came to work after those all-nighters, I would do drugs on my lunch break to help me get through the rest of the day. Sometimes, I would nap in my office.

Not long after my friend's death, I started dating a fellow who had also been my cocaine connection. We were both stunned by her death and used our new relationship as a vehicle to hide from the rest of our circle of friends. We stopped going to the bar, stopped doing drugs, and became pretty much consumed with each other. After about a year of this, we started to head back to our favorite bar and socialize. He liked cocaine, but he snorted it. He didn't like that I shot it. I couldn't help myself. I tried to get help in order to save the relationship. I realized that I couldn't do cocaine without eventually shooting it, and I couldn't drink without eventually doing cocaine. It all had to go, and I needed help to do that. Somehow, I got connected with 12-step groups. I attended meetings once a week. I made no connection with people outside of the meetings and followed none of the suggestions I heard at the meetings. I continued to go to bars, continued to hang out with the same people, and thought that being sober meant not being drunk. (That is, if I could just keep it to one drink, I was still sober.) I stayed away from cocaine for about three months, during which time I had one drink on Thanksgiving and one drink on New Year's. It was not long before I was drinking without restraint and doing cocaine. I met someone who introduced me to smoking cocaine. I liked smoking cocaine and thought that this would help me to stay away from the needle. It wasn't until someone asked me how long I'd been freebasing that I realized I was still in trouble. I became just as out of control with smoking cocaine as I'd been with shooting it, and ultimately my preference was still injection. By now, AIDS was becoming a very real scare. I'd learned of all the ways to sterilize a needle in order to prevent AIDS, but when I wanted to get high, I wasn't willing to take that extra time. This also helped me finally hit bottom. There was no way to treat AIDS at that time, yet I repeatedly risked infection. I couldn't help myself. This scared me.

I was readmitted to Rutgers in 1988. I really wanted to do well academically this time, yet I found I would often fall asleep in class. I sought counseling through student counseling services. My counselor suggested I might have a problem with drugs. She presented me with the notion that addiction is a disease, not unlike diabetes, in that it is not a personal failing but something that can be managed effectively with the right treatment. This was a new concept to me. Yet, I still felt that, if I could just give up the needle and deal with some childhood issues, I'd be okay. This counselor suggested I try attending 12-step meetings. I told her I'd tried that and found those people and their meetings to be rather cult-like. I wasn't interested. She gave me a phone number and suggested I call it. I don't know what I thought this number was for, but I called it. A woman answered the phone saying something about Alcohol and Drug services. I cringed, but I made an appointment. I kept the appointment, and this became my glimpse of a new beginning.

I started attending individual and group sessions on a weekly basis at the Rutgers student treatment program. I was still resistant to total abstinence and 12-step meetings. I did not know anyone who didn't drink. My counselor got me to agree to try their suggestions for a 90-day trial period. I met another student at one of the groups who invited me to meet her at an AA meeting. I started attending AA and NA meetings regularly. Something started to click. I started to realize that there was a way out from the way things had been. It had been a year since the last time I'd attended 12-step meetings. During that year, I had, at times, tried to get clean by reading literature alone in my room. It didn't work. As cliché as it sounds, I really had become sick and tired of being sick and tired. This was not the worst period of my addiction. My life had become relatively tame. But I wanted to stop doing cocaine altogether, and I couldn't for any length of time. Likewise with my drinking; though it was not always out of control, I often set limits for my drinking that I was unable to keep. I really can't explain why this was the time that I got sober; it just was.

I struggled with the words *alcoholic* and *addict*. I believed that an alcoholic was an old man in a trench coat who hadn't shaved, lived on the street, drank out of paper bags every waking moment, and smelled bad. This wasn't me. I believed that a drug addict was someone who sold their appliances, stole, and prostituted. This wasn't me. Part of the shift that occurred as I got sober was that I began to stop staring so hard at the stereotypes that didn't apply to me, and I began to explore the consequences I'd experienced as a result of my use of alcohol and other drugs. I started to recognize that not being able to quit when I wanted to, going out for one drink and staying to close the bar, driving in blackouts, flunking out of school, going to work after being out all night, and putting myself in unsafe situations are all indications of how my life was out of control, signs of powerlessness and unmanageability in my life.

Once I started to experience some freedom from alcohol and other drugs, I started to worry about losing it. I knew how quickly I could slip back into my old patterns. I took to heart all the suggestions that I had ignored the first time. I gave up the bars, went to meetings every day, and stopped hanging around with my old friends. It wasn't easy. The bar I went to was the hub of my social life. I truly felt that my friends were more than just drinking buddies. But I came to realize that, if I was serious about this, being around them was a threat to staying sober. This was no reflection on them. Getting high is what they did, what we have always done together. For me, I needed to break that pattern. I told my friends that they could come see me at a meeting if they wanted to. I wasn't trying to convert them to my way of life, but I knew that meetings were a safe place for me. I also invited friends to come to AA dances with me. I had some friends who were comfortable doing this and others who weren't. Rutgers was opening a dorm for students in recovery, and my counselor suggested I move into it. Though my roommates were rather tame, they did drink and smoke pot on a somewhat regular basis. I can't say they had a problem, but at the time, I felt that being around this was a threat to my staying clean and sober. Their use of alcohol and other drugs made it look socially acceptable and fed into that part of me that still wanted to think it was okay for me to do this. I was not eager to move into a university apartment. I'd lived off campus for about six years. Moving back on campus and sharing a room with someone felt like a step backward. But I decided that it was a step I needed to take to give my sobriety a better chance. My roommates understood and were very supportive. I am grateful for this. And I feel that I made the right decision. In this apartment, I was surrounded by people who were in recovery. We went to meetings together, we socialized together. This setting provided me with support similar to a halfway house without the stigma and restrictions.

My grades actually declined some after I got sober, no doubt because I was going to meetings every night and hanging out with people after the meetings. It was a worthwhile sacrifice. My grades were still far from a 1.3, and my attendance and performance were consistent. I had three semesters to complete in order to finish my Bachelor's.

Once I opened up to this process of recovery, I was like a sponge. That doesn't mean I didn't question things, but I was open and receptive to the process. During one of my first groups, a peer vented about how he really didn't want to be there. This was liberating for me to hear. I didn't think it was okay to admit that. When I first tried going to meetings, I often sat there wishing I could get high, but I didn't think I could say that. Now I realize that I need to say that. If I feel like getting high, I have to talk about it. I don't need to entertain the thought, but I need to share the feeling. I've learned that there's usually something else behind the feeling, and the desire to get high is just a desire to escape. Once I acknowledge that desire, I can get to what's really the issue. If I act on that desire, I'm gone.

The first time I had a really strong urge to drink was after final exams. This caught me totally off guard. I had finished the semester and wanted to celebrate. The only way I knew how to celebrate was to go drinking. I called a number of people on my phone list until I found someone available to talk. I met her at a meeting a few hours later. I just needed to get through that initial impulse, and then I was okay. I carried a phone list with me everywhere I went for quite a while. I remember being away for a training weekend for work and calling people from a pay phone because I wanted to drink. I got answering machines, but hearing their voices was a comfort to me. Making the calls allowed me to put enough space between the impulse to drink and the action that I stayed sober. I read daily meditations, I read 12-step literature, I attended daily meetings, I did service work, I surrounded myself with recovering people, I journaled, I went to therapy. I had gotten a taste of something that I was so afraid to lose, and I knew all too well how easily I could lose it.

I'm a very practical person, and if I was going to go to meetings every night, I felt that I should understand why. I eventually had to give up trying to understand why they helped me and just accept that they did. I still felt that there was a somewhat cultish quality to the meetings; all the clichéd sayings and group responses were weird. I eventually accepted that perhaps there is a cultish quality, but I had been brainwashed for years by my addiction to believe that everyone drinks, and that drinking and getting high are a normal part of life and adolescence. So if these people were brainwashing me into being sober, what did I really stand to lose? Today, I've come to see some of the rote practices of 12-step groups as perhaps a de-programming. The culture of intoxication is usually very ingrained in those of us who come to 12-step groups for help. We need a lot of repetition and routine to break through years of conditioning. One persistently redeeming element for the 12-step groups is that there is an openness that clearly distinguishes them from a cult. Though there is a spiritual factor to the steps, it is clearly "a higher power as you understand it." And it is common practice that you have the freedom to "take what you can use, and leave the rest behind." Cults don't give you these options. I did not initially agree with everything I heard in meetings. There are still some things I don't entirely agree with. It's okay for me to question things. Sometimes questioning has helped me come to a personal understanding about something. Sometimes questioning has helped me to realize that not everything is meant to be understood.

I learned that insanity is "repeating the same thing and expecting different results." If the last time I went out for one drink I ended up closing the bar and spending all my money, what made me think this time would be different? I began to explore the notion of a power greater than myself. I was not very comfortable with traditional religion. I heard someone say once in a meeting that they called their higher power "Sam" because the one thing he knew for sure was it "Sure Ain't Me." I could relate to this. I began to develop a strong faith that there is a force in the world that is wiser and greater than I am. I began to see miracles in everyday life, like someone sharing at a meeting about how they overcame a problem that I was currently silently struggling with. I struggled with the idea of turning my will and my life over to anyone or anything. But when I thought about it, I had to realize that I had been turning my will and my life over for years, to the force of my addiction. So what did I really stand to lose to turn my life over to a positive force? The 12 steps have become a framework for how I approach many aspects of life today. The first three steps have provided a foundation for all the work I've done since.

I quit smoking cigarettes when I had almost a year sober. I completed my Bachelor's and have gone on to get a Master's degree. I have spent the last 15 years working in mental health and substance-abuse counseling.

Drinking and getting high is not an option for me. I have had my heart broken in recovery. I have experienced the death of family and friends in recovery. Though I was spared HIV infection, I have battled other chronic illnesses in recovery. Today, I know down to my bones that there is no crisis that drinking would resolve. I have learned other ways to handle stress, or escape if necessary. Ways that don't have negative consequences.

Last night, I went to a viewing for a friend from recovery. He had a wife, family, and, at one time, about 10 years of recovery. The last time I saw him, he had just gotten out of rehab and was really struggling. This reminds me why I still go to meetings. I do have a disease. I have effectively managed it for 17 years, with a lot of help. I have seen too many other people with 10, 15, 20 years clean and sober go back out and die from this disease. That little voice is still waiting to chime in with "just one won't hurt," "you deserve it, you've worked hard," and "no one has to know."

I am very grateful for the angels who came in to my life while I was at Rutgers. As crazy things may have been, they would have had to get a lot worse before I would have considered interrupting my life to go away to rehab. Rutgers allowed me to continue with my day-to-day life while also immersing myself in treatment. I was 25 when I got sober. I was able to get sober surrounded by other young people, other students. I was able to keep that piece of my identity while I sorted out the rest. I will be forever grateful to Rutgers for that, and I try to remember the gentleness I experienced in the work I do with people today.

Chapter 11

I Never Identified

. . . she never felt like she fit in, even within her own family.
Alcohol helped until it didn't help anymore, and her life didn't get better
until she found recovery.

I grew up in a loud, energetic household in a small town in New Jersey. I was the youngest of four girls and have a brother three years younger than me. My three oldest sisters were close in age, and they did many things together. When they were in their late teens/early 20s, they frequented bars and had house parties and beach house shares. Their social life seemed glamorous, and I couldn't wait to be accepted into their circle when I started experimenting drinking in seventh grade. Unfortunately, regardless of my drinking, I was still too young and immature to be a part of their crowd. From the start, I never felt like I fit in, even within my own family.

The same feelings carried over for the next 10 to 15 years. In high school, I wasn't very athletic, wasn't a cheerleader, but I always seemed to fit in when it came to partying. When my classmates were concentrating on getting ready for college, I was too busy worrying about beer money and the social circuit to care about anything significant. Along with the secretarial jobs that I had after graduation came all of the firings that I had to cover up because I just couldn't handle the partying, with the alarm clock and the commute. I soon found my niche: I began to bartend! Sleep all day, party all night. My so-called friends soon outgrew me because I was a fly-by-night friend. If you weren't doing something that I was interested in, which basically was, if you weren't interested in where I wanted to drink on my nights off, then I'll find someone else to hang out with. I conveniently married my schoolmate's older brother, who happened to DJ where I was bartending. Side note, we never really dated, just drank, etc., together. We moved to Hoboken, where we were working, so that it was safer to get home at the end of the night. I burned more bridges there because of my Jekyll & Hyde personality. My husband and I started college; I was 23 at the time.

On campus, I was continuously in and out of the nurse's office at the clinic. I was always sick, needing antibiotics from running my body down (drinking and socializing all hours of the night and fitting in a marriage with schoolwork). She gave me a tuberculosis skin test because of an epidemic on another campus. Test turned out positive; I was exposed to TB. I was required to take medication for this for six months, with heavy restrictions on drinking because of the liver. This was October. I told her that I would take the medication right after the New Year. She insisted that I begin the medication that day, and I insisted on getting through the holidays (Halloween, Thanksgiving, Christmas, and New Year's). How could she possibly expect me not to drink during the holiday season! She made an appointment for me with the drug and alcohol counselor upstairs. How dare she? Meantime, I reluctantly began the medication, but couldn't even make the six months. During the fifth, I conveniently forgot to take the bottle on vacation, and started my drinking again. Because I was now seeing this counselor weekly, and also attending a sober student group once a week, the drinking between that April and October of 1993 was anywhere from controlled due to negative guilty feelings.

It was Mischief Night, October 30, 1993. I was waitressing at the restaurant and had a group of "friends" from school come in and wait for me to finish up. They were 19 years old; I was 27, trying to be 19. First stop was a bar called Bahama Mamas. People who live in Hoboken don't hang out there; it's a weekend touristy kind of bar, one that we make fun of their patrons (they give out leis and straw hats and play really corny music). I think I was having a good time there; I was dancing with Henry, the "town bum," who, before that night, I despised. Later, we left and went to the club where my husband was DJ'ing. I proceeded to tell him about dancing with Henry earlier and also had my last drink.

The next morning, I woke up in the usual manner: throwing up over the side of the bed, begging God to remove the feelings from me, and promising never to drink again. When Mike began to fill me in on the events of the night (blackouts were the norm) and came to the part about Henry and I dancing together, I got down on my knees, admitted that I don't drink normally, that maybe those sober students were right, and asked for help.

I would like to say that's where my sobriety starts, but I was a bit thick-headed. It took a few months before I felt comfortable enough walking into an Alcoholics Anonymous meeting, and I truly believe that I may never have gotten there if it weren't for an old friend, who happened to have served me my last drink where my husband was working that night. Her name is Jill, and she was also attending Rutgers. We ran into each other a few times, when I would brag to her that I wasn't drinking (didn't tell her that it was due to the medication). She got sober shortly after me. In June of 1995, I was asked to speak (for the first time) at my Saturday morning home group. The night before, I couldn't sleep a wink. I kept going over in my mind an incident that happened on St. Patrick's Day 1994. My husband and I were on a cruise, and I was "dry" for four and a half months. I felt so guilty that I was such a boring wife because I couldn't drink that I convinced him that it was okay for us to enter a beer-chugging contest. Thank God that I had some sort of a moment of clarity because when I put that beer to my lips and felt the carbonation, I jerked it away, and pretty sure (hindsight) that not a drop made it past my mouth. At that Saturday morning meeting, I admitted about my half-relapse and changed my sober date from Halloween '93 to St. Pat's Day '94. So far, no one has disputed the date, and the Irish in me celebrates on the 17th and not the 18th!!!

Okay. Final part of my story. I was (and still am) a

meeting maker. And for a while, that was ALL that I was. I had a sponsor in name only, a home group that I never took a commitment at, and never had a sponsee who stayed sober. You can't give it away unless you have it!!! I was never shown "precisely how to stay sober," as outlined in our "Big Book."

I never learned anything about turning my will over, never took inventory, never asked God to remove the defects that I NEVER IDENTIFIED, and never cleaned house with a formal amends! During my fourth year, I was divorced and miserably living with my boyfriend. I was speaking with a guy who was new to our area at a meeting. I found it easy to speak with him about my feelings of sober life, the "is that all that there is" blues. He asked me what steps I was focusing on, and I guess I was a deer in headlights. I admitted to him that I had no clue as to the meaning or benefit of the steps. He brought me to a meeting in New York that his sponsor from Florida suggested that he go to. From there, I found a true sponsor, someone who was going to sit me down and take me through the book, starting at the title page, and show me how to write out my fourth step inventory when it was time to do so (after the groundwork of the first three steps were in order). Some of my amends have been the most rewarding experiences in my life. I flew down to Florida to make an amends to my ex-husband. I made a really humbling amends to my father. My ex-husband is someone very important in my life today, and I can be there for him as he's separating from his wife and kids. And my father has now moved in with me after he and my mother split up and sold the house last year. The rewards are countless, thanks to my sponsor, my awesome home group, and a loving higher power whom I turn to each day to help me get through the trials and humbly thank at day's end for another day of not having to rely on a drink to make my life livable.

Chapter 12

Ha-Ha, We Have Her Now!

. . . she drank differently from everyone in her family and discovered other differences while in rehab.

My name is Karen, and I am an alcoholic. I am the middle child of three; all of us are girls. My mother and father were married the day after Christmas in 1960. I am proud to say that they are still happily married after all these years. Both of my sisters are also happily married. For the most part, I grew up in the "Brady Bunch"; that is not to say that all of our problems were solved in 30 minutes, but there was a lot of communication and love, growing up in our household.

Neither of my parents is a heavy drinker. I have no memory of my father ever being drunk. My mother falls asleep after two glasses of wine, so here's a novel idea: She'll have only one glass when she has any at all. My sisters, on the other hand, have been known to overindulge; however, alcohol has not presented the same problem for them as it did for me. Of course, growing up in an Italian family, there was always wine at holiday dinners. My sisters and I were allowed a small glass on these special occasions.

When I was almost four years old, my grandparents on my father's side and my parents bought a two-family home in Bayonne, New Jersey. We lived on the first floor, and they lived upstairs. At dinner, my grandfather would take a fresh peach, slice it up, and put the slices into a hi-ball glass. He would then pour red wine into the glass and let the peaches soak. He would sip at the wine through dinner, and then eat the peaches as his dessert. This ritual would occur every night, except during Lent.

He would give up his wine and peaches every year at Lent because he was a good Catholic.

If there is a history of alcoholism in my family, it would be my grandfather on my mother's side. My image of him is him in his recliner with a pack of Bel-Air cigarettes and a bottle of Seagram's-7 on the coffee table next to him. However, as a child, I was not exposed to my grandfather's drinking. My grandparents lived in Jersey City, and when we would go to visit, if my mother realized my grandfather had been drinking, we just didn't stay long. My mother has since told me stories of how my grandfather would get drunk; throw my grandmother, my mother, and her siblings out of the house; then wonder where they were in the morning.

So, excluding my one grandfather, I come from a pretty "normal" family. Then there's me. My mother has often said that I walk to the beat of a very different drummer, and when she gets her hands on him, he has a lot of explaining to do. From day one, I was different. Everyone in my family was born on the East Coast. Both of my parents were born in Jersey City, New Jersey; my older sister in Dover, Delaware; and my younger sister in New Brunswick, New Jersey. I was born on the West Coast. My Dad was in the Air Force, and we were stationed near Tacoma, Washington. My sisters were typical girls. I, on the other hand, was very much the tomboy. I much preferred to play Wiffle Ball than have anything to do with Barbie. My sisters were popular in school, and I was a loner. My best friends were my books and a tennis ball I would throw against the garage wall. Somewhere along the line, I had gotten the message that I was not good enough. I am not sure exactly when or where, but I distinctly remember feeling different and less than.

My first drink outside of my parents' supervision was during the summer between seventh and eighth grade. I was hanging out with a group of friends at the end of my block. There were six of us, and someone's brother, or cousin, or uncle had bought us a six-pack of beer. It is the only time in my life that I can honestly say that I had only one drink. I sipped that bottle of beer the entire night. I hated the taste of it, but it was the first time I felt like I fit in, that I was just like everyone else. That's what alcohol did for me. It made feel like I belonged.

I drank throughout high school, mainly on the weekends. My drinking was very controlled because I had to be sober enough to be able to talk to my parents when I got home. The only time I ever got caught drinking, I had tried to bypass the nightly, "So where have you been" conversation, and instead made a beeline for my room. My mother stopped me halfway down the hall, and asked if I had been drinking. There was no point in lying, so I told her yes. She asked me how much, and I answered "Two." She said, "Well, for a person who doesn't drink, two beers is an awful lot." I had meant two six packs.

I kept the extent of my drinking hidden from my parents. I excelled in school and graduated in the top five percent of my class. I was accepted at Rutgers College in New Brunswick, New Jersey, and started my freshman year in September of 1983. Since I lived on campus, I no longer had to answer to my parents—and my drinking took off. I went from being an "A" student to barely passing. I would simply rather party than study. I also joined a sorority in my first semester. In the world of fraternities and sororities, the alcohol was free and flowing. So while they had raised the drinking age back to 21, I had no problem getting alcohol. When my parents asked about my grades, I told them that college was harder than I had expected, and promised to bring my grades up next semester. At the end of my freshman year, my grandfather on my mother's side passed away. I remember being very angry with him because I had to miss the end of year party at my sorority to attend his wake and funeral.

I spent the summer back in Bayonne, living with my parents and telling my friends I was going through "frat party withdrawals." When I got back to Rutgers in September of 1984, my drinking, of course, took off again. In mid-September, all of the fraternities and sororities hold rush week to try and recruit new members. On the last night of rush, I went to my sorority house and started drinking there. A group of us then went down the street to a fraternity that was having their annual "golf" party. They would set up nine different rooms with nine different drinks. They even gave you a little "scorecard" when you walked in the door. The idea was that you would go from room to room, and drink "par" for the room, which was either two drinks or three shots, depending on the drink. Initially, I was going to have a few drinks, head back to my sorority house to find out about the new pledge class, and then go home because I had a rugby game in the morning. However, after having a couple of drinks in the first room, I decided that this whole golf thing sounded like fun. And, hey, you never know; they may not have this party next year.

After the fourth or fifth room, I vaguely remember somebody stopping me and telling me I had hit a "sand trap." In order to get out of the "trap," I had to eat a piece of fruit that had been soaking in grain alcohol for a week; again, it sounded like a great idea. I spent the rest of the evening in and out of blackouts. I remember leaning over a pool table at one point and having someone from the rugby team ask if I was going to be able to play the next day. I said, sure, no problem.

Somehow, I made it back to my sorority house. I was later told that I proceeded to get sick in the bathroom for two hours. One of my sorority sisters, Stephanie, was trying to help me; and to thank her, I took a swing at her. I missed and hit the bathroom wall instead. As I came out of my blackout, I found myself sitting on the couch in the living room, talking to yet another sorority sister. She was saying that if I ever needed to talk to anyone, she was always there for me. I had no idea what she was talking about. With that, Stephanie came into the living room and said she was going to call a friend to come and take me home. I had no intention of leaving; I was not done drinking yet. So, I did what any drunk would do, I took a flying leap off the couch and attempted to tackle her. Again, I missed. With that, six of my sorority sisters pinned me to the floor. They were insisting I was drunk, and that I needed to calm down. I told them they were crazy and that I was stone cold sober. Someone threatened to call the police if I didn't relax. I called her bluff and said, "Go ahead." Much to my amazement, she did. The police showed up, took one look at the situation, and called the paramedics. The paramedics came in with leather restraints. It was at that moment that something in my brain clicked, and I knew that I had better calm down. I relaxed, the paramedics got me into the ambulance, and I immediately started to sob.

They took me to the Emergency room, drew some blood, and basically let me sleep it off. My only concern, at that point, was that my parents should not be notified. When I signed myself out of the hospital, the doctors told me that there had been enough alcohol in my system for two people my size to be drunk. When they had gotten back the blood test, they had been amazed that I was alive, let alone conscious. And this was after being sick for two hours. I left the ER, made it back to my apartment, took a shower, and headed to my rugby game. I played in the game but felt like I was a step behind everyone. After a rugby match, it is tradition to go back to someone's place, get drunk, and sing dirty rugby songs. It is the only time I can remember ever turning down free alcohol. Instead, I went home and slept the rest of the day.

Because this whole incident had taken place in a sorority house, the Dean of Fraternities and Sororities had been notified. She wanted to talk to me. I thought for sure that I was going to be thrown out of school. I kept thinking, great, how am I ever going to explain this to my parents? I went to her office, and, much to my surprise, she said all I had to do was contact the director of the University Recovery Program and all would be forgotten. The program was a recovery program for students who had problems with alcohol and drugs. I tried to call her. I really did. I think I got as far as dialing the number and letting it ring once before hanging up. Then one afternoon, my phone rang. I picked it up, and it was the director. She said she had a very interesting police report on her desk and wanted to know if I would like to come in and talk about it. I agreed and actually showed up at the appointment.

The director gave me one of those 20-question quizzes that is supposed to tell you if you have a drinking problem. Well, I either passed or failed with flying colors, depending on how you look at it. The director said that I MIGHT have a drinking problem. In my head this translated to I MIGHT NOT have a drinking problem. She asked me if I was still drinking. I told her I was but that I had it under control. She said okay, but that if I got into any more trouble, we would have to try things her way. She also asked me if it was okay to give my phone number to another student, Lily, who was also in this recovery group. I said, sure, no problem.

Lily actually called me. We talked on the phone, and she suggested I go to an AA meeting. For some strange reason, I agreed. I like to tell people that I was kidnapped to my first AA meeting, because Lily and another student named Irene picked me up on a Friday after rugby practice. Irene had a little two-door Chevy Chevette. I got into the back seat, and then Irene and Lily looked at each other and said, "Ha, ha! We have her now!" I thought, great, what have I gotten myself into? They took me to an open AA discussion meeting for young people. It was on the second floor of a church parish house in New Brunswick, New Jersey. There were about 15 people sitting around this conference table, drinking coffee. They went around the room and introduced themselves, and when it got to me I said, "Hi, my name is Karen, and I think I might have a problem with alcohol, and that's why I am here." They all smiled and told me to keep coming. After the meeting was over, we went back to Lily's apartment, talked for a couple of hours, and then I promptly went over to my sorority house, had a couple of beers, and went home.

The following week, I went back to that meeting. To this day, I am not sure why. No one called me to tell me I should go. No one forced me to go back there. For some reason, I just went. I do remember not having anything to drink that Friday. Probably because when they said, "Don't drink and go to meetings," I thought they meant you shouldn't drink before going to a meeting. When I walked through the door, Lily said "hi" and asked if I was still drinking. I thought, what a silly question, and told her that of course I was still drinking. She then suggested I not drink for 90 days. I told her I couldn't do that because it was the annual "Fall Back Weekend" at my sorority and tonight we were having a party. She said that, if I wasn't an alcoholic, 90 days would be easy and that my parties would still be there. Now, I am a very logical thinker, and I really couldn't think of a good argument to her reasoning. So, I agreed to not drink for 90 days and prove that I wasn't an alcoholic. That was October 12, 1984, and I haven't had a drink since. I was 19 years old at the time.

I continued going to that Friday night meeting as well as other meetings. I continued to introduce myself by saying I thought had a problem with alcohol and that was why I was there. People at the meetings just kept smiling and telling me to keep coming. About a month or so into proving that I wasn't an alcoholic, I introduced myself by saying, "Hi, my name is Karen, and I am an alcoholic." Everybody applauded, and I immediately wanted to take it back, but I just kept coming back.

I also was still hanging out at my sorority house because I simply refused to change people, places, and things. At about six months, I was at the sorority house helping to set up for a party—rolling in kegs of beer, decorating the house, etc. After setting up, I was waiting for some folks to pick me up to go to an AA meeting. While I was waiting, two of my sorority sisters came in and asked if the keg was tapped. Being the good alcoholic, I said "no" and volunteered to tap it for them. We headed down into the basement. I tapped the keg, poured three glasses instead of two. They took their beer and went back upstairs, leaving me alone with the keg and the extra glass of beer. You see, the keg wasn't quite tapped right, so I was attempting to fix it. In the process, beer had gotten all over my hands. Then that glass of beer started talking to me. Who would know? It would be only ONE glass of beer. I WAS heading to a meeting. Then, just as I was about to reach for the glass, I heard

111

my friend, who was picking me up to go to the meeting, call from the top of the stairs. I ran up the stairs, and out to the waiting car. My friend made me roll down the window and stick my hands out of the car. I was in rehab that following Wednesday.

When I first got to rehab, I had to fill out a questionnaire. One of the questions asked if you had any problems with your sexual identity. Without a second thought, I checked "No." During my 35 days in rehab, one of the gifts I received was being put on the "hot seat." Basically, a group of my peers got to take my inventory. This was supposed to help me deal with any last-minute issues that might threaten my sobriety once I left the safety rehab. As they went around the circle, the one thing being repeated was, "You have a secret, and you need to face it." When I heard this, I would say, "okay," but I was clueless about the secret they were referring to. Finally, one woman directly asked me if I was gay. I looked at her and simply said, "I don't know." Up to that point, I had never really thought about it much. I had dated boys throughout high school and in college. I didn't quite understand what the big deal was about sex. I think on some level I knew there was something different about other women and me when it came to men. After this hot-seat session, my counselor asked me why I hadn't told her that I was having an issue with my sexuality. I told her because when I came into rehab, I wasn't having an issue. I simply wasn't aware of it.

I was fortunate enough to be surrounded by people who did not judge me. When I left rehab, I returned to Rutgers, and found a place to rent off campus. I started therapy with a counselor, was involved with the recovery program and went to meetings. I also found gay AA meetings as well. Coming out as a lesbian was relatively easy for me. It was like an old V-8 commercial, where the actor hits himself in the head, and says, "Oh! I could have had a V-8!" Coming out was pretty much the same way for me, "Oh! I'm a lesbian!" And I was off to the races. I was involved in my first lesbian relationship when I was 10 months sober. She was also in recovery, but our relationship lasted only a few months. I have had several relationships in recovery, some successful, others complete disasters. But from each experience, I have always learned something new. All of which has led me to the relationship I have now. My partner, Kathy, has been sober for over eight years. We both work hard at our sobriety and our relationship. It isn't always easy, but recovery has taught us both how to work at it one day at a time.

I think that's what recovery has really been about for me. Over the past 20-plus years, I have been able to chase my dreams, one day at a time. Since I was nine years old, I had talked about becoming a truck driver. When I was eight years sober, I finally went to driving school and got my Commercial Driver's License. I drove 18-wheelers cross-country for three years and then regionally for two years. I came out to my family and have been very fortunate that my parents love me and accept my partner, even though they don't understand. At 12 years sober, I went back to school to pursue another passion: computer programming. I received a certificate and landed a great job as a mainframe programmer, eventually making more money than I had ever imagined. Three days after starting my new career, my first niece was born, and I was able to be there. I have learned what it means to have true friends and not just drinking buddies. At 16 years sober, my second niece was born, and my sister asked me to be her godmother. I have bought and sold homes and cars in recovery. I have gotten into debt and somehow pulled myself out of that miserable hole. At 19 years sober, I had the opportunity to speak at the "Big" meeting at an AA conference. Then in June 2004, my grandmother died. About two weeks later, and after having worked for the same company for six and a half years, I was fired because I lost my temper and yelled at a co-worker in front of other people. I learned that, no matter how long I stay sober, I still had work and growing to do in recovery. Kathy and I had also decided it was time for us to chase yet another dream: moving to Maine. We packed up our things, said good-bye to our friends, moved to the coast of Maine to be closer to Kathy's mother, and pursue a career in the arts. We found that there really are no strangers in AA, only friends

113

you haven't met yet. And, more importantly, I have learned that, as long as I don't drink, one day at a time, anything is possible.

Made in the USA
Middletown, DE
12 July 2015